THE POEMS OF LAURENCE MINOT 1333–1352

edited with select contemporary materials, notes, and an introduction

by

THOMAS BEAUMONT JAMES
and
JOHN SIMONS

UNIVERSITY OF EXETER

1989

ISBN 0 85989 234 4

We dedicate this edition to undergraduates at King Alfred's College
who helped us to resurrect Minot
and his contemporaries.

Printed in Great Britain by BPCC Wheatons Ltd, Exeter

THE POEMS OF LAURENCE MINOT

EXETER MEDIEVAL ENGLISH TEXTS AND STUDIES
General Editors: Marion Glasscoe and M. J. Swanton

PREFACE

In preparing this edition we have incurred numerous debts and received help without which it would have been difficult to complete the project successfully. Thanks are especially due to Bob Perkins for his dedicated work on the translation of the Latin poems in Appendix 2, to Chris Given-Wilson who read the manuscript and made many helpful suggestions, to Alex Turner who prepared the map, to Stanley Matthews and Alasdair Spark for constant advice on the technicalities of refining text on a word-processor, and to Kate Downhill who drew the cover illustration. We also acknowledge the assistance of cultural attachés at the Belgian and French embassies in solving a topographical problem and of King Alfred's College for help in meeting certain incidental expenses connected with the preparation of this edition. The library staff at King Alfred's have been, as ever, unstinting in their assistance. Finally, thanks are due to Professor Michael Swanton for his encouragement throughout the project.

TBJ and JS
Winchester
July 1988

CONTENTS

Introduction to the Poems of Laurence Minot

EDITIONS

The purpose of this edition is two-fold. First we aim to make easily available a text of the poems of Laurence Minot which will facilitate access to this unique figure. No edition has appeared since 1917. Secondly we wish to demonstrate the value of collaborative enterprise in teaching and scholarship which seeks to open up medieval culture as an inter-disciplinary field and to break down some of the barriers which now traditionally separate the enterprise of the literary critic and the historian. This enterprise takes place against the background of Minot's fluctuating reputation, for while few readers would now agree with the verdict of the first editor Joseph Ritson (1795 and 1825) that:

> In point of ease, harmony, and variety of versification, as well as general perspicacity of style, Laurence Minot is perhaps equal if not superior to any English poet before the sixteenth century, or even, with very few exceptions the seventeenth century,

the decay of Minot's reputation to the point where he is now only known to a handful of medievalists and then only as an oddity may need redress. The late Professor J.A.W. Bennett (1986, p. 395) provided a modern opinion:

> It is rare for poems such as these, however topical in their own time, to live on to engage the interests of later readers.

This may be true of much political poetry. However, we have found that in the context of an inter-disciplinary course on the Anglo-Scottish wars of the early fourteenth century and the subsequent Hundred Years War between England and France (1337-1453) Minot's poetry has engaged the interest of students. The poems provide an ideal bridge across which the mutual determinations of history and culture may be seen to shuttle.

However much modern scholars may distance themselves from Joseph Ritson's view of Minot's work, the poet would have no doubt remained even more obscure but for the splash with which Ritson relaunched the poems towards the mainstream of English literature. His detailed work on the poet, which in the first edition ran to some 50 pages of introduction and nearly 200 of text, glossary and notes, might be thought to have been over-enthusiastic as a response to Minot, stimulated by the then recent rediscovery of the poems by Tyrrwhitt. However, thirty years later, in 1825, Ritson produced a new edition developing his previous ideas, and in this edition the statement, printed above, about Minot's place in English literature is repeated. The revival of medieval studies and the Romantic Movement fuelled interest in the Gothic and helped promote Ritson's work: Minot's poetry was to be found on the shelves of many contemporaries including the romantic poet Robert Southey, whose personal copy is now in the British Library. Subsequently, Minot was to find a place in Thomas Wright's *Political Poems and Songs Relating to English History from the Accession of Edward III to the reign of Henry VII* (Volume 1, 1859), part of the second wave of publications in the Rolls Series which began with a veritable flood of material in 1858.

There it might be thought interest in Minot would have rested, but it was not to be. Enthusiasm for both the historical development and geographical spread of the German language was no doubt heightened by the unification of Germany in 1870. Not surprisingly, then, it was a German edition of Minot, edited by Scholle which appeared in 1874 under the umbrella of (and as a very small component in) the philologist Ten Brink's *Quellen und Forschungen zur Sprach- und culturgeschichte der germanischen Völker* (1874-1918).

- 2 -

INTRODUCTION

What was to become the most well known English edition first appeared in 1887, in the Clarendon Press Series of English Literature begun in 1866. The editor on this occasion was Joseph Hall, a scholarly Lancashire headmaster. Ritson and Wright, but latterly Scholle and especially Hall, guaranteed Laurence Minot a place in a further grand late-nineteenth century work of reference, the *Dictionary of National Biography* (1885-1900), which was in progress when Hall's first edition was published. Joseph Hall's work went to a second edition in 1897 and a third edition in 1914. Each edition was marginally larger. Hall's editions are the versions of Minot most commonly seen today. It was this edition which was used in the twentieth-century revival of interest in the middle ages by, amongst many others, C.S. Lewis whose personal copy, with marginal pencillings from Hall's excellent glossary, was sold not long ago. The most recent edition of Minot to appear followed hard on the heels of Hall's last printing when Douglas C. Stedman published *The War Ballads of Laurence Minot* in Dublin in 1917.

It may be dangerous to speculate on motives for editions of Minot, but hindsight may be helpful. Ritson's work had a variety of stimuli, most obviously the recent rediscovery of the poems. Also Ritson was challenged to be Minot's first modern editor by Tyrrwhitt's assertion that Edward III 'had not the gift of discerning and patronizing a great poet' (Ritson 1795, p. vi). In editing Minot, Ritson created the court poet of the king who had given Chaucer a post in the customs (provided he wrote the accounts with his own hand), but gave him no preferment at court for his writing. In any case we now believe that Chaucer's writing would have come too late to catch the ailing Edward's attention. Other influences on Ritson would have included the vogue for Gothic and subsequently Romanticism. In addition the fervour which followed the French Revolution of 1789, and the subsequent Napoleonic Wars harked back to the medieval Anglo-French conflicts which are the focus of Minot's work. German nationalism, and the nineteenth-century passion for codification helped to keep Minot if not in the public eye then at least on the shelf of scholar and student.

INTRODUCTION

The continuing popularity of Hall's editions for upwards of a quarter of a century after 1887 is testimony to that great age of scholarly interest in the middle ages and chivalric values. These values were questioned by those who survived the Great War. Stedman's edition (1917) may have arisen not so much from the anti-French or antiquarian interest which had attracted his predecessors, as from the flowering of poetry in World War I. Stedman established the idea familiar to late twentieth-century readers of Minot as a 'war poet.' In 1917 Minot's Poem IX, line 6:

> The flowres that faire war er fallen in Fraunce

would certainly have had a peculiar poignancy. The next we hear of Minot was the 1920 publication by Sam Moore of documents relating to land transfers in the name of a certain Laurence Minot, maybe our poet, in 1329 and 1331 (Moore 1920, pp. 78-81; see below). The significance of Moore's discoveries lay in the unearthing, for the first time other than the poems themselves, of materials which refer by name to a contemporary Laurence Minot. Moore's work is a but a small flag which signals the changing direction of historical and literary studies at that time.

In recent years Minot has been cast in different roles from those wished upon him by earlier commentators; major literary figure (Ritson) or nationalist poet (Wright and Hall). Carolyn Collette (1971, p. xxx) praises Minot as the first poet to use the English language for a series of poems although her main thrust is in the directions of language and style. In 1974 John Barnie reminded his readers of Minot's prayer for peace at the end of his poem on Halidon Hill, a rare cry against war in the literature of the Hundred Years' War (Barnie 1974, pp. 40-1; Poem I, lines 91-2):

> Jhesu, for thi woundes five,
> In Ingland help us to have pese.

Insofar as the war was fought largely on French soil, Minot might argue that his prayer was answered.

INTRODUCTION

This edition, some two centuries after the rediscovery of the poems and almost exactly a century after Hall first went to press, gathers up the threads of twentieth-century work on Minot, looking at his poems from the now distinct perspectives of literary and historical scholarship. With our expressed aims of providing an easily available text and of bridging the history - literature gap, it follows that this little edition will attempt only to provide a good reading text, produced by a re-transcription of the manuscript and checked against other editions, and such critical and historical apparatus as is needed to help the reader find a context for the poetry. We wish to present Minot as a figure of literary and historical significance rather than as a philological curiosity, so the linguistic and palaeographical data and the analysis of metre which the reader might reasonably expect to find in a grander undertaking are absent here. Materials for such a study may easily be culled from our select bibliography.

THE MANUSCRIPT

The poems of Laurence Minot may be found in an unique copy in Ms. Cotton Galba E. Ix. This is a neatly written parchment manuscript which appears, on the evidence of handwriting, to date from the early fifteenth century, about fifty years after the composition of Minot's final verse. Its unfussy hand and simple decoration indicate the work of a competent, professional production team and any thoughts on Minot should start with a consideration of the codicological environment and historical context of his poems for from this a critical exposition of their form may be started.

As a collection Cotton Galba E. Ix. contains two romances (*Ywain and Gawain* and *The Seven Sages*) much pietistic material (including a copy of that most common of all medieval texts *The Prick of Conscience*) and some political and historical material. Appendix 3 lists the contents of Galba E. Ix. Thus if we consider the manuscript as a whole book we find a not unusual blend of material for a late medieval compilation which mixes the secular with the religious and the chivalric with the pious. It is certainly significant that Minot's poems should appear with other less systematic versifications of political and historical events. Perhaps, though, it is no less significant that an author whose style shows him to have been thoroughly steeped in the lexis and ethos of the Middle English romances (couplet, stanzaic and alliterative) should also appear in a volume whose commissioner or compiler plainly saw some natural relationships between the material. From a critical viewpoint this is important because it signals how in the Middle Ages it was not possible firmly to separate the record of history from the narrative of fiction. Indeed, to this day, the term 'history' retains an ambiguity which fossilises a lack of discursive division. The English language alone preserves separate words for 'history' and for 'story', which further contributes to the fortification of specialisation in the plain of academic study. What are now separate ways of thinking happily jostle together in the medieval codex. The historian and the critic, so familiar to twentieth-century readers, were indistinguishable to the medieval mind. So when we read Minot, we should not expect to find an accurately documented account of Edward III's campaigns but rather a harmoniously organised version of them which arranges the exciting events using an appropriate literary mode: the chivalric romance.

Before moving to examine the poet in his fourteenth-century milieu, we might dwell a moment on the historical considerations which arguably surrounded an early fifteenth-century copy of the poems. Merlin's prophesies are to be found both in the Minot poems and elsewhere in Galba E. ix. In Minot Poem VII, lines 1-2, 7-16:

> Men may rede in romance right
>   Of a grete clerk that Merlin hight;
> ....
> Merlin said thus with his mowth,
>   Out of the north into the sowth
> Suld come a bare [boar] over the se
>   That suld mak many man to fle;

INTRODUCTION

And in the se, he said ful right,
   Suld he schew ful mekill might;
And in France he suld begin,
   To mak tham wrath that er tharein;
Untill the se his talle reche sale.
   All folk of France to mekill bale.

In Galba E. ix. a further prophesy of Merlin is used to discredit Henry IV's claim to the throne, and contrasts strikingly with the exaltation of the prophesy of the boar, Edward III, who was in Minot's day so triumphant in France. Galba E. ix. is usually dated on internal evidence to the period of Henry IV's reign before 1407. The usurper-king certainly enjoyed public support at the outset of his reign, and the battle of Shrewsbury (1403) crushed the Percys, and reminded others who might contemplate baronial opposition to the king of the strength of royal power. By 1407, and perhaps from 1405, Henry was a sick man suffering a form of nervous prostration, brought on by pressures of state. One of these pressures was his failure to pursue war against France. After all, Richard II's moves towards peace and his marriage to a French princess in 1396 had been high on the list of reasons for his deposition. The sending back of the princess (but not of her dowry) after the usurpation had re-awakened Anglo-French antipathy at the highest level. Hopes of a successful war against a France weakened and divided by the rule of the mad king Charles VI (r. 1380-1422) had been dashed, and in Galba E. ix., in particular in the juxtaposing of Merlin's prophesies, we see flashes of discontent boldly committed to paper and neatly copied up for posterity.

Not all authorities agree on a date in Henry IV's reign. The edition of *Fourteenth Century Verse and Prose* (1921 rp. with corrections 1971), by Kenneth Sisam, dates Cotton Galba E. ix. to *c.* 1425. Such a date could accord well with the same considerations set down for Henry IV's reign. In the 1420s, following the death of Henry V in 1422, and of Charles VI in the same year, the joint kingship of England and France passed to the infant Henry VI. His uncles acted as regents in the baby's stead, John Duke of Bedford in France and Humphrey Duke

of Gloucester in England, with the assistance of Cardinal
Beaufort. In Henry V's reign, and even after Agincourt, the war
party had needed such propaganda as 'The Libelle of English
Policye' to maintain military momentum. By 1425, despite
Bedford's steady successes in France (before the tide turned at
Orleans in 1429), and Humphrey's warlike posturings at home, a
peace party was well established, led from the start of the
reign by Cardinal Beaufort. Although we might not expect one
of Gloucester's documents to have ended up in the Cotton
collection, this avid collector and bibliophile might possibly
have been original owner or might have commissioned Galba E.
ix., including Minot, to strengthen the war party in
increasingly difficult times. Against this speculation may be
placed the name Richard Chawser which is to be found at the
end of the manuscript. This may well be the signature of an
early owner of Galba E. ix., although the hand seems to be of a
later date. It was this signature which probably led the
Chaucerian editor Tyrrwhitt to inspect the manuscript in the
late eighteenth century.

THE POET AND THE COURT OF EDWARD III

There has been much speculation on the identity of Laurence
Minot. The evidence suggests that he came from Yorkshire
though Norfolk and Lincolnshire have also been mooted (Pearsall
1983, p.129). The language of the text is certainly northern
but this of course may be scribal rather than authorial since
the language of other pieces in the collection exhibits
northern features. However, while genealogical materials exist,
it seems impossible that a final answer will be found in the
present absence of appropriate documentation (See *DNB*; Moore
1920). Perhaps it is more profitable to ask 'What was he ?' To
this question some probable solutions can be propounded.

Minot's poems are unambiguous eulogies to the prowess of
Edward III — mentioned some 50 times in 1000 lines — and an
account of the iniquity of his enemies the French and the
Scots. It may be therefore, that it is at the court of Edward

INTRODUCTION

III that our speculation on Minot should begin. While it has often been thought that Edward's circle was rather dourly military and that splendour at court took a rather low place in the list of this soldier-king's priorities, recent work has shown that this was not the case and that the court thrived under his tutelage. However, Edward's court seemed to have had an interest in the almost old-fashioned nostalgic form of chivalric writing. This form contrasts strikingly with the modern and increasingly Italianate forms which were to become predominant in the gorgeous world of Richard II and this interest is significant for our understanding of Minot.

In this respect the work of Judith Vale is indispensible and her analysis of the record of issues and receipts of books maintained by John Fleet, Keeper of the Privy Wardrobe at the Tower, enable her to conclude that there was 'a sustained pattern of literary interest in this milieu throughout the reign of Edward III' (Vale 1982, p. 51). This milieu was Edward's immediate family and closest courtiers and in such detail were the records kept between 1322 and 1341 that we can pick out chivalric romance as a dominant thread in the reading pattern of the courtly circle. Indeed, not only did Isabella the queen mother borrow romances but ten *'libri romanizati'* were among her goods when they were inventoried on her death in 1358.

Edward himself is well known for his interest in reviving chivalric festivals but, as Vale points out, the ewer which Philippa of Hainault presented him at New Year 1333 and which was enamelled with various chivalrous heroes, reflects 'the familiarity of Edward and his household with a wide range of *Chanson de geste* and romance figures' (Vale 1982, p. 45). At the same time Philippa was plainly known as a patron and Jean de la Mote addressed his lament on the death of Guillaume de Hainault to her. As Vale points out:

> even if Philippa did not offer de la Mote permanent employment it was evident that he was sufficiently convinced of her literary interest to feel it worth his while to address her. (Vale 1982, p. 45)

The more celebrated Froissart was luckier and did gain patronage. Surprisingly, it was for poetry rather than prose that he first won attention, but, coming back to Minot this only confirms the suspicion that his verses form part of chivalrically-oriented literary vogue centred on the court and a personal desire for patronage.

It is reasonable to see Minot in this context as very far from a minstrel or balladeer whose verses achieved sufficient currency to gain the accolade of being recorded and whose name as an oral performer has come down to us by a quirk of history. Instead he should be seen as one amongst the increasingly large retinue of minor functionaries who thronged the later medieval courts and who decided to seek preferment through the production of laudatory poetry in a style which may have appealed to the king himself. Laurence Minot was not a poet who followed the usual course of anonymity in his writing, for he records his name twice in the course of his eleven poems, to impress his identity on the reader (or the hearer). Unfortunately there speculation comes to an end, for we have, so far, no documentary evidence which decisively identifies Minot in this or any other environment. The only tantalising scraps are a patent roll deed and an entry in the Receiver of Ponthieu's account book of what appears to be the same land transfer, recording a purchase of land in Cressy (Crecy) Forest (Ponthieu) in 1329 by one Laurence Minot (Laurence Mynotz, Loreng de Minguot) and the remission by Edward III in 1331, of a part of the price still unpaid.

On the question of court patronage for Minot we are again in the realms of pure speculation. Three leading possibilities suggest themselves. First Edward III himself: he is the central character and romantic hero in the poems. References to 'our king' and the warmth of praise mark Edward out in this respect. In addition there is the land transaction between a Laurence Minot and the king, recorded in 1331. Secondly there is Philippa of Hainault, the queen, a keen patron of writing, attracted to Froissart initially by his poetry and his main supporter in his 'English period' of chronicle prose.

INTRODUCTION

There is a third possibility: the old queen, Isabella (d. 1358). In 1329 when Minot bought into it, Crecy Forest was in her hands; it reverted to Edward III in 1331 on his mother's fall from power. The king dealt kindly with Minot, taking into account the collapse of the value of the money owed on the land. Isabella's interest in romances is well attested in her inventory and her career encompasses all the events alluded to in the poems (from Bannockburn, 1314 to Guines, 1352) as well as all the known references to Laurence Minot(s) (1329-1352). In addition we know that despite her association with Mortimer and acquiescence in the murder of Edward II, she revived a good relationship with her eldest son Edward III, who arguably named his eldest daughter Isabella, in her honour as his eldest son Edward the Black Prince (a figure conspicuous by his absence from Minot, when compared with Dauphin John) was presumably named after Edward II. Accounts of Isabella's bad character have been exaggerated. In any case Edward III provided her with a good income for her retirement at Castle Rising (Norfolk), a county with which the Minots had strong associations. Whatever she thought, as the last of the Capetians, of the disasters which befell France in the 1340s and 1350s, she had much cause to be proud of her eldest son and no doubt supported his claim to the French throne, a claim which came through her. It would be cynical to argue that Edward III's good opinion of his mother derived from her precipitation of his accession to the throne, and thus the performance of the heroic deeds celebrated by Minot. We shall never know, but the beginning of Minot's work in 1333, when the queen mother had leisure to reflect, and the tactful reference to the redeeming of her late husband's disastrous defeat at Bannockburn by the victory at Halidon Hill, might encourage us to look to Isabella as a potential patron of our poet. These three are not the only patrons available to Minot, who names in his poems a number of others in the royal circle in a way reminiscent of Froissart, with whom he has much else in common.

STYLE AND CONTENT

The poems describe events which span the years 1333-1352. They are not scrupulously accurate in detail but narrate significant events at this period in Edward's war against Scotland and France. Because Minot employs a range of style culled from the Middle English romances he has been branded a minstrel following the critical tendency to identify the traces of minstrel composition in the longer narrative form. Scholle's reference to L. Minot's *Lieder* (1874) exemplifies this line of thinking. It is worth saying that the evidence for such composition is supposition, based on a projection from style and runs against the clear material existence of codices of romance which bear the marks of selection and arrangement which we would normally term literary. This is not to say that romances were never read aloud, only that they are literary rather than an oral, and that traces of minstrel style such as the call to attention or generalised formulaic diction should be considered the conventional features of a genre.

Thus the poems of Minot are full of formulae which crop up throughout the corpus of Middle English romance in all its varieties. Certainly anyone familiar with the romances will see that they have more in common with Minot's verses than do lyrics although lyrics more nearly match in length. However, remembering the importance of a text's physical environment (for that is where the first readers saw it) we should consider the effect of reading Minot's poems not as isolated ballads, but continuously as they are copied. If we do this we find a text of some 1017 lines, a length which compares very favourably with that of the shorter romances, and which takes some twenty minutes to half an hour to read out loud. We also find a text which presents an almost continuous narrative sweep of the chivalric adventures of a hero Edward and his conflict with Philip of Valois, the notable gap being the failure for any obvious reason to mention the Brittany campaign of 1342-3. Philip VI, together with his son John, as the narrative progresses, achieve considerable stature as incorrigible villains. The fifty or so references to Edward (usually supported by God) are nicely balanced by an almost

Identical number of references first to Philip of Valois, and increasingly to his son John, who assumed the crown of France, and thus the heightened opprobrium of the English, following Philip VI's death in 1350.

We are not suggesting that this was a conscious mode of composition but rather that, in the context of one medieval book the experience of reading Minot would have been analogous to the experience of reading a short romance, divided into fitts, with appropriate features and generic markers and satisfying the expectations which romances generally fulfilled. The text is thus far from a collection of isolated celebrations but an attempt to unify disparate experiences over a lengthy period through the deployment of an easily recognisable and currently fashionable literary mode. Above all we find an image of patriotic heroism and foreign villainy, an image reflected not in a mirror of chronicle but in a mirror of chivalric romance.

Minot's poetry dates from a twenty year period of the fourteenth century. The first poem relates to the battle of Halidon Hill (1333) and the last poem to the siege of Guines (1352). The second poem, on Bannockburn (1314), was apparently written in the wake of the English triumph at Halidon Hill, seen as revenge for the defeat at Bannockburn. Exactly when Minot wrote each individual poem remains a matter of debate. Clearly the surviving manuscript records all eleven together. However there is some internal evidence to suggest that they were probably written down separately near to the time of each event, as for example, the siege of Tournai which records the siege independently of the knowledge that Edward summarily raised the siege and left the city. Thus it can be argued on the one hand that Minot was there, but left before the siege was raised and so restricted himself to writing about what he had witnessed. On the other hand he may never have been near Tournai, but may merely have arranged known facts to suit his poetic purpose. Such selectivity is a common device in military reporting, as was noticed by Morris in his analysis of soldiers songs of a slightly earlier period (Morris 1947, *passim*). Also, as Chris Given-Wilson suggests, the reference to the *duke* of

Lancaster, in Poem V (line 41), points to a date of writing after 1351 when Henry of Grosmont became a duke and thus argues for a late compilation, or revision of the poems. Arguments have raged to and fro about whether or not Minot was present at any or all of the events he describes. The evidence reads in different ways. We now know of a Laurence Minot associated for a time at this period with lands in Ponthieu; if he collected the revenues himself he must have been to France. In the case of the sack of Southampton, he states, against the evidence from other authorities, that Edward III was there. Taken together the evidence implies neither man was there in 1338, especially not Minot who gets into a muddle over the capture of the 'Cristofer.' This and other evidence adds up to a good deal of uncertainty, of the kind to be expected in attempts to draw conclusions from internal evidence.

The point about the topics chosen by Minot is that, for whatever reasons, they were the military happenings in the first twenty years of Edward III's personal rule which one contemporary thought significant. Historians, employing their professional shorthand, tend to isolate certain events as 'important.' The battle of Crecy was one such event. However, contemporaries, bearing in mind the unscheduled nature of the encounter at Crecy (however triumphant the outcome), might have liked to dwell on other aspects of the war: the curtailing of Scottish pretensions at Halidon Hill, the carefully orchestrated siege and capture of Calais, the destruction of Franco-Castilian sea forces at Sluys and off Winchelsea. Such an interpretation might help explain the inclusion of the final poem on the capture of Guines. This was not a royal campaign, but a spirited piece of free enterprise involving John of Doncaster. The town was subsequently sold by the captors to Edward III. Why was this affair included ? Some have suggested it appealed to Minot because he had been a witness; others that the bravery of Doncaster (elsewhere described as an archer of Calais) appealed to Minot's Yorkshire spirit, if the poet did come from Yorkshire. Another possibility might be that the poet, like contemporary chroniclers, liked to draw attention to the potential of the war to make a personal profit and to gain royal approval, funds and renown, even in time of truce. In the last resort we shall never know whether or not Minot saw what he described. What is certain, as Philippe Contamine points out (Palmer 1981, pp. 132-44), is that although Froissart did not witness a fraction of what he described he conjured up *'grâce à la vivacité de son imagination et à l'étendue de sa curiosité les lacunes de son information ainsi que son manque d'expérience directe de la guerre.'*

The years from 1333-1352 enjoy an historical unity, representing an almost unbroken era of English military success on a broad land front, from Scotland and Flanders to France, and including naval encounters. The outbreak of the Black Death in 1347 in France and the following year in England, made a natural break in official hostilities; Winchelsea and Guines being unofficial encounters in 1350 and 1352. What is puzzling is the omission of the Brittany campaign of 1342-3, and here it is possible only to fall back on the suggestion that there may have been a lost poem. Although Edward was to lead a great, and what is now seen to have been comparatively ineffectual, expedition through northern France in 1359, a new phase of military leadership by the Black Prince had opened with a flourish at the battle of Poitiers in 1356. In addition the personal struggle between Edward III and Philip VI, who had initially set aside Edward's claim to the throne of France, had ended with the death of Philip in 1350 and the accession of his son as John II (r. 1350-1364).

In the Introduction to his editions of Minot's poems Joseph Hall stated that Minot's 'direct historical value is small' apart from the occasional curious detail. The poet's main claim on the attention of posterity is that 'he is the abstract of the spirit of his time, its undoubted bravery, its glitter, its savagery, its complete absence of pity for the conquered.' Minot's verses' 'greatest merit lies in their warm and spontaneous expression of national feeling ...... he is the first [poet] to speak in the name of the English nation just awakened to a consciousness of its unity and strength' (Hall 1897, p. xlii). The statement of the paucity of Minot's historical value contains a grain of truth: there are only occasional scraps of evidence to be found in Minot which are not to be found in contemporary chroniclers. There are numbers of inaccuracies, but no one would deny the significance of Froissart's account of the fourteenth-century wars for all his many errors. Thus we are left with Minot as 'the abstract of the spirit of his time' and herein - apart from in his prime position as the earliest writer of a series of English poems - lies his real value.

Minot, like Froissart but to a much less marked degree, has suffered at the hands of the 'scientific historians' of the late nineteenth and twentieth centuries. John Palmer's impressive effort to re-establish Froissart's declining reputation opens with a timely reminder of the dangers to the likes of Froissart and Minot from the scientific historians:

> Volumes have been devoted to the analysing of the mistakes it [Book I of Froissart] contains, and practically the only serious works of modern historical scholarship which have failed to add to its list of errors of chronology, geography and genealogy are those which have elected to ignore it entirely. (Palmer 1981, p. 7).

Minot's former editors have ploughed the furrows of comparison of poetic with chronicle accounts of the events mentioned in the verses, including the unreliable Froissart, on whom Ritson depended almost entirely. It is not the purpose of the present editors to enter again into such detailed analysis, which as study of Froissart has shown can be a remarkably circular exercise. It can be said with some assurance that modern scholarship based on administrative sources has offered more reasonable answers to certain questions, for example about sizes of armies, than the huge hosts of 120,000 and more, accepted as a realistic English force by earlier editors. The *Société de l'histoire de France* began a line by line analysis of Froissart's *oeuvre* in 1869. This massive work is still in progress.

The spirit of the two decades following 1333 (with the brief account of Bannockburn, 1314) is captured in a variety of ways.

INTRODUCTION

Clearly at the centre is the character and performance of the king of England himself, set against the leaders of the French (Poem IV, lines 88-90):

> Sir Philip of Fraunce fled for dout,
> And hied him hame with all his rout;
> Coward, God giff him care.

War at sea and on land is described; Sluys (1340), Crecy (1346) and off Winchelsea (Espagnols sur Mer) (1350) as well as civilian misery; the sack of Southampton (1338) and the siege of Calais (1346-7). Siege warfare is highlighted at Guines (1352). Individual acts of bravery are credited, such as that of 'Gentill John of Doncaster' at Guines, who launched a single handed attack on foot against the great castle. The geographical spread of the war, from Scotland through England, Flanders, and France to Gascony is brought into focus in different episodes. Virtually the whole potential range of combatants and mediators is to be found: Scots, English, French, Brabanters, the Holy Roman Emperor, Lewis the Bavarian, and the Blind King of Bohemia, Genoese mercenaries, French cardinals and so on. The references to the French as 'normans' and especially the reference to the 'fals folk of Normundy' are worthy of note, as they seem to echo a fear, current in the thirteenth and early fourteenth centuries that the Normans, who had conquered England in 1066, were eager to repeat their success. The hatred of John II as the Duke of Normandy, a recurrent theme in the poems, may have arisen from similar apprehensions.

The poems are full of action and the bustle of campaigning comes brilliantly down the years (Poem IV, lines 79-81);

> The princes that war riche on raw,
> Gert nakers strike, and trumpes blaw,
> And made mirth at thaire might

The cruelty of action against civilians is signalled by Minot in his setting of the scene for the siege of Southampton by the Franco-Castilian fleet (Poem III, lines 53-6):

He [Philip VI] comand than that men suld fare
Till Ingland and for no thing spare
Bot brin and sla both man and wife
And child, that none suld pas with life.

Edward's campaigning abroad led to some speculation that he had mistresses in France (as, in later life he was to have in England), particularly during the year long siege of Calais. Minot captures in passing a flavour of not only the dangers, but also the temptations, of campaigning (Poem IV, lines 10-13):

And Mari moder of mercy fre,
Save our king and his menye
To sorow and schame and syn.

The eleven poems printed here largely speak for themselves in recalling the wars between England, France and Scotland as they were fought not only on land and sea, but also on paper. The kind of nationalist, or propagandist, writing found here is matched - indeed surpassed - in contemporary chronicles. Nor, surprisingly, compared with contemporary invective is Minot's tone overly strident (see Appendix 2). Let us not forget that while Minot praised Edward for his military leadership and kingship, Jean le Bel recorded the story of Edward's alleged rape of the Countess of Salisbury (attributed to 1341), and John of Fordun entered in his *Scotichronicon* the story that Edward knifed to death his younger brother John of Eltham in a brawl during a church service at Perth in 1336 !

Chronological Table

1286   Death of Alexander III of Scotland.

1290   Margaret of Norway, his heiress, drowned.

1291–2   Edward I involved in adjudication of claims to the Scottish throne. John Balliol not Robert Bruce (d. 1295) is chosen by the jury. Potential Scots civil war, English intervene.

1295–1305 Anglo-Scots war. English success, William Wallace executed.

1306   John Comyn of Badenoch, nephew of John Balliol, killed by Robert Bruce (Poem I, line 77). Bruce crowned king as Robert I (r. 1306–29).

1307   Death of Edward I (r. 1272–1307). Accession of Edward II (r. 1307–27).

1314   Scots victory at Bannockburn 23–4 June (Poem II).

1316   On the death of Louis X the French invoke Salic Law to declare that no woman may inherit the throne of France (see 1328).

1320   Declaration of Arbroath, Scots lords vow independence from England.

1323   Thirteen year Anglo-Scottish truce.

1324   Treaty of Corbeil asserts Franco-Scottish 'auld alliance'. Minot (Poem I, lines 25–8) pronounces that the French promised much and did nothing.

1327   Deposition and death of Edward II. Accession of Edward III (r. 1327-77).

1328   Treaties of Northampton and Edinburgh (*'Turpis pax'*) embody English recognition of Scottish independence. Scottish kings receive papal dispensation to receive unction at coronations.

Death of Charles IV (r. 1322-28) last Capetian king of France. The French invoke Salic law and choose Philip VI (r. 1328-50), a cousin of the Capetians, not Edward III, son of Charles IV's sister, Isabella who is ruling England with Roger Mortimer. On this occasion it is argued that a claim to the throne of France may not be transmitted through a woman (see 1316) in order to rule out not only Edward III but other potential claimants.

1329   Death of Robert I (the Bruce). Accession of David II (r. 1329-71), regency during David's minority, to 1341. Succession question reopened.

1330-1   Overthrow of Isabella and Mortimer. Execution of Mortimer, enforced retirement for Isabella. Edward III's personal rule begins.

1332   Thomas Randolph, Earl of Moray and regent of Scotland dies. Edward Balliol, English-backed claimant to the Scottish throne invades and wins the battle of Dupplin Moor (Perth) and is crowned king of Scotland. John Randolph, Earl of Moray, drives Balliol out (Poem I, line 42).

1333   19 July, battle of Halidon Hill (Poem I). Decisive English victory over Scottish relief force attempting to raise the siege of Berwick. English employ tactics later highly effective in France of fighting dismounted with archers on the wings of the army. Edward III and Balliol set about conquest of Scotland.

1337   Anglo-French Hundred Years War begins.

1338   16 July Edward III sailed from the Orwell for Flanders, arriving on 22 September at Antwerp. Met the Holy Roman Emperor, Lewis of Bavaria (r. 1314-46) at Coblenz (Poem III).

              French raid south coast of England and sack Southampton (4 October) (Poem III, line 59ff). The 'Cristofer' captured by the French (Poem III, line 75ff).

1339   Edward III in Flanders. 23 October, battle of Flamengerie (Poem IV).

1340   24 June, battle of Sluys (Poem V). This resounding victory over French naval forces probably ensured the war was fought on French rather than English soil. A French invasion plan was later captured at Caen (1346).

              Siege of Tournai, July to September (Poem VI). Edward III unable to continue to support his allies financially lost such support as they had promised, abandoned the siege and returned home leaving Philippa and his baby son John virtually as hostages at Ghent. Treaty of Esplechin sealed in September. Edward's expenditure on his allies had been far beyond his means and the treasury was empty. The king tried to gain extra funds and blamed Archbishop Stratford for incompetent financial management of the realm. In truth Edward's campaign was under-financed; the king failed to prove his charges against Stratford who was supported by his parliamentary peers against the king.

1346   (Poem VII). Edward III led an expedition with the apparent aim of sailing to Gascony. However he was diverted by contrary winds to St Vaast-le-Hogue (Cotentin) and marched through Normandy with a

French army in pursuit. Despite some considerable success the English found themselves heavily outnumbered by the French army and were probably aiming for a haven in Flanders when they were brought to battle at Crecy (26 August), which proved to be a decisive English victory.

Thereafter Edward settled down to beseige Calais which fell in the late summer of 1347 (Poem VIII).

During these English preoccupations in France, the Scots invaded England under David II, but were defeated decisively at Neville's Cross near Durham on 17 November, where David was injured and captured (Poem XI).

1347-9   Black Death in Europe and then Britain. Truce between the major combatants, broken on occasions by unofficial encounters such as at Winchelsea and Guines (Poems X and XI).

1350   Death of Philip VI, accession of John II (r. 1350-64). Castilian fleet defeated off Winchelsea in the battle known as 'Espagnols sur Mer' (Poem X).

1352   Capture of Guines by the English, probably in January (Poem XI).

1356   Battle of Poitiers. Focus of the war moves to the south of France, until Edward III's great expedition through northern France in 1359.

Location Map

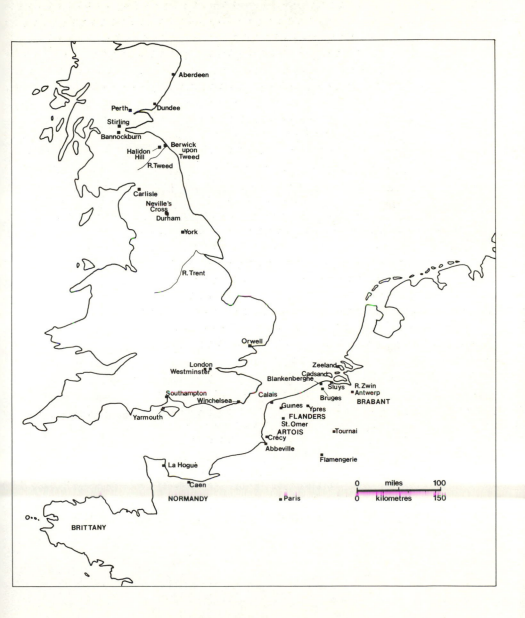

Map of places mentioned in the text

Capet/Valois Descent and Claimants to the Throne of France

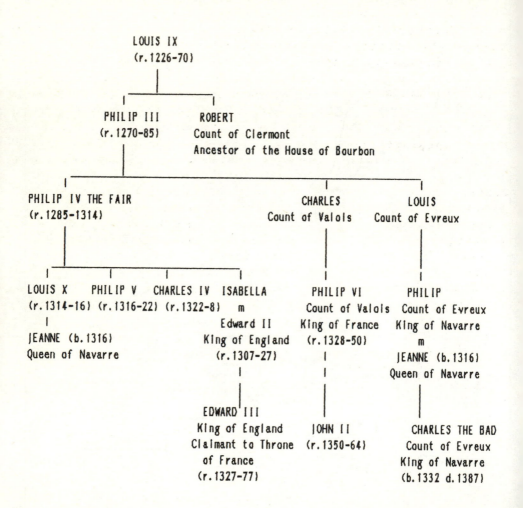

LOUIS IX
(r.1226-70)

PHILIP III
(r.1270-85)

ROBERT
Count of Clermont
Ancestor of the House of Bourbon

PHILIP IV THE FAIR
(r.1285-1314)

CHARLES
Count of Valois

LOUIS
Count of Evreux

LOUIS X   PHILIP V   CHARLES IV   ISABELLA
(r.1314-16)   (r.1316-22)   (r.1322-8)   m
                                             Edward II
JEANNE (b.1316)   King of England
Queen of Navarre   (r.1307-27)

PHILIP VI
Count of Valois
King of France
(r.1328-50)

PHILIP
Count of Evreux
King of Navarre
m
JEANNE (b.1316)
Queen of Navarre

EDWARD III
King of England
Claimant to Throne
of France
(r.1327-77)

JOHN II
(r.1350-64)

CHARLES THE BAD
Count of Evreux
King of Navarre
(b.1332 d.1387)

THE POEMS OF LAURENCE MINOT

I

52r Lithes and I sall tell yow tyll
(a)   The batalle of Halldon Hyll.

Trew king, that sittes In trone,
    Unto the I tell my tale,
And unto the I bid a bone,
    For thou ert bute of all my bale.   remedy, woe
5 Als thou made mideLerd and the mone   earth
    And bestes and fowles grete and smale,
Unto me send thi socore sone
    And dresce my dedes In this dale.   guide, world

In this dale I droupe and dare   hide
10   For dern dedes that done me dere.   dark, harm
Of Ingland had my hert grete care
    When Edward founded first to were.   went
The Franche men war frek to fare   eager
    Ogaines him with scheld and spere,
15 Thai turned ogayn with sides sare,
    And al thaire pomp noght worth a pere.   pear

A pere of prise es more sum tyde   value, time
    Than all the boste of Normondye.
Thai sent thaire schippes on ilka side
20   With flesch and wine and whete & rye.
With hert and hand es noght at hide
    For to help Scotland gan thai hye:
Thai fled and durst no dede habide,
    And all thaire fare noght wurth a flye.   boast

25 For all thaire fare thai durst noght fight
        For dedes dint had thai slike dout;   death's stroke/such fear;
    Of Scotland had thai never sight
        Ay whils thai war of wordes stout.
    Thai wald have mend tham at thaire might   acted
30   And besy war thai thareobout.
    Now God help Edward in his right,
        Amen, and all his redy rowt.

    His redy rout mot Ihesu spede
        And save tham both by night and day;
35 That lord of hevyn mot Edward lede
        And maintene him als he wele may.
    The Scottes now all wide will sprede
        For thai have failed of thaire pray;
    Now er thai dareand all for drede   hiding
40   That war bifore so stout and gay.

    Gai thai war and wele thai thoght   relied
        On the Erle Morre and other ma;
    Thai said it suld ful dere be boght
        The land that thai war flemid fra.   put to flight
45 Philip Valays wordes wroght
        And said he suld thaire enmys sla;
(b) Bot all thaire wordes was for noght,
        Thai mun be met if thai war ma.

    Ma manasinges yit have thai maked,   menaces
50   Mawgre mot thai have to mede   bad luck,reward
    And many nightes als have thai waked
        To dere all Ingland with thaire dede.   harm
    Bot, loved be God, the pride is slaked   diminished
        Of them that war so stout on stede
55 And sum of tham es levid all naked
        Noght fer fro Berwik opon Twede.

A litell fro that forsaid toune
    Halydon hill that es the name,
Thare was crakked many a crowne
60   Of wild Scottes and alls of tame:
Thare was thaire baner born all doune;
    To mak slike bost thai war to blame: such
Bot never the les ay er thai boune   ready
    To wait Ingland with sorow and schame.   harm

65 Shame thai have als I here say;
    At Donde now es done thaire daunce,
And wend thai most another way
    Evyn thurgh Flandres into France.
On Filip Valas fast cri thai
70   Thare for to dwell and him avaunce;
And no thing list tham than of play   It pleased
    Sen tham es tide this sary chance.   happened

This sary chaunce tham es bitid,
    For thai war fals and wonder fell;   fierce
75 For cursed caitefes er thai kid   known
    And ful of treson, suth to tell.
Sir Ion the Comyn had thai hid,
    In haly kirk thai did him qwell;   kill
And tharfore many a Skottis brid   woman
80   With dole er dight that thai most dwell. appointed

Thare dwelled oure king, the suth to saine,
    With his menye a litell while;   company
He gaf gude confort on that plaine
    To all his men obout a myle.
85 All if his men war mekill of maine
    Ever thai douted tham of gile;
The Scottes gaudes might no thing gain, tricks
    For all thai stumblide at that stile.

Thus in that stowre thai left thaire live   place
   That war bifore so proud in prese.   battle
Ihesu, for thi woundes five,
   In Ingland help us to have pese.

II

Now for to tell yow will I turn
Of the batayl of Banocburn.

52v Skottes out of Berwik and of Abirdene,
(a)   At the Bannok burn war ye to kene,
   Thare slogh ye many sakles, als it was sene   Innocent
    And now has king Edward wroken it, I wene,   avenged
5 It es wrokin, I wene, wele wurth the while;
   War yit with the Skottes, for thai er ful of gile.

Whare er ye, Skottes of Saint Iohnes toune ?
   The boste of yowre baner es betin all doune;
   When ye bosting will bede sir Edward es boune   ready
10   For to kindel yow care and crak yowre crowne:
   He has crakked yowre croune, wele worth the while;
    Schame bityde the Skottes, for thai er full of gile

Skottes of Striflin war steren and stout;   stern
   Of God ne of gude men had thai no dout;
15 Now have thai, the pelers, priked obout;   thieves
   Bot at the last sir Edward rifild thaire rout,
   He has rifild thaire rout, wele wurth the while,
   Bot ever er thai under, bot gaudes and gile.

Rughfute riveling, now kindels thi care,   rough brogue
20   Berebag with thi boste, thi biging es bare   house
Fals wretche and forsworn, whider wiltou fare?

Busk the unto Brug and   abide thare;
Thare, wretche, saltou won and wery the while;   live
   Thi dwelling in Donde es done for thi gile.

25   The Skotte gase in Burghes and betes the stretes,
   All thise Inglismen harmes he hetes;   vows
Fast makes he his mone to men that he metes,
   Bot fone frendes he findes that his bale betes
Fune betes his bale, wele wurth the while,   few
30   He uses all threting with gaudes and gile.

Bot many man thretes and spekes ful ill
   That sum tyme war better to be stane still;
The Skot in his wordes has wind for to spill,
   For at the last Edward sall have al his will:
35   He had his will at Berwik, wele wurth the while;
   Skottes broght him the kayes, bot get for thair gile. look

I I I

How Edward the king come in Braband
And toke homage of all the land.

God that schope both se and sand   made
   Save Edward king of Ingland,
Both body, saul and life,
   And grante him ioy withowten strif:
5   For mani men to him er wroth

In Fraunce and in Flandres both:
   For he defendes fast his right,
And tharto Ihesu grante him might,

And so to do both night and day,
10 That yt may be to Goddes pay.   satisfaction

(b) Oure king was cumen, trewly to tell,
  Into Brabant for to dwell.
 The kayser Lowis of Bavere,
  That in that land than had no pere,
15 He and als his sons two
  And other princes many mo,
 Bisschoppes and prelates war thare fele many
  That had ful mekill werldly wele,
 Princes and pople, ald and yong
20 Al that spac with Duche tung,
 All thai come with grete honowre
  Sir Edward to save and socoure,
 And proferd him with all thayre rede, advice
  For to hald the kinges stede.
25 The duke of Braband, first of all,
  Swore, for thing that might bifall,
 That he suld, both day and night,
  Help sir Edward in his right,
 In toun, in feld, in frith, and fen; forest
30 This swore the duke and all his men
 And all the lordes that with him lend
  And tharto held thai up thaire hend.
 Than king Edward toke his rest
  At Andwerp, whare him liked best
35 And thare he made his mone playne money
  That no man suld say thare ogayne;
 His mone that was gude and lele,
  Left in Braband ful mekill dele;
 And all that land untill this day
40 Fars the better for that iornay.
 When Philip the Valas herd of this
  Tharat he was ful wroth, I wis;
 He gert assemble his barounes caused to
  Princes and lordes of many tounes.
45 At Pariss toke thai thaire counsaille
  Whilk pointes might tham moste availe;

And in all wise thai tham bithoght
   To stroy Ingland and bring to noght.   *destroy*
Schipmen sone war efter sent
50   To here the kinges cumandment;
And the galaies men also   *galley*
   That wist both of wele and wo.
He cumand than that men suld fare
   Till Ingland and for no thing spare
55 Bot brin and sla both man and wife   *burn*
   And childe, that none suld pas with life:
The galay men held up thaire handes
   And thanked God of thir tithandes.   *news*
53r At Hamton, als I understand,
(a)   Come the galayes unto land,
61 And ful fast thai slogh and brend,   *burned*
   Bot not so mekill als sum men wend;   *much*
For, or thai wened, war thai mett
   With men that sone thaire laykes lett. *games/ended*
65 Sum was knokked on the hevyd
   That the body thare bilevid;   *stayed*
Sum lay stareand on the sternes   *stars*
   And sum lay knokked out thaire hernes: *brains*
Than with tham was none other gle,
70   Bot ful fain war thai that might fle.
The galay men, the suth to say,
   Most nedes turn another way;
Thai soght the stremis fer and wide
   In Flandres and in Seland syde.
75 Than saw thai whare "Cristofer" stode
   At Armouth opon the flude,
Than went thai theder all bidene   *together*
   The galayes men with hertes kene,
VIII and xl galays and mo,
80   And with tham als war tarettes two,
And other many of gallotes,
   With grete noumber of smale botes;
All thai hoved on the flode
   To stele sir Edward mens gode.
85 Edward oure king than was noght there
   But sone when it came to his ere,

He sembled all his men full still
   And said to tham what was his will.
Ilk man made him redy then,
90   So went the king and all his men
Unto thaire schippes hastily
   Als men that war in dede doghty.
Thai fand the galay men grete wane   plenty
   A hundereth ever ogaynes ane;
95 The Inglis men put tham to were   war
   Ful baldly with bow and spere;
Thai slogh thare of the galaies men
   Ever sexty ogaynes ten,
That sum ligges yit in that mire
100   All hevidles, withowten hire,   pay
The Inglis men war armed wele
   Both in yren and in stele;
Thai faght ful fast both day and night
   Als lang als tham lasted might;
105 Bot galay men war so many
   That Inglis men wex all wery:
(b) Help thai soght, bot thare come nane;
   Than unto God thai made thaire mane.
Bot, sen the time that God was born
110   Ne a hundreth yere biforn
War never men better in fight
   Than Ingliss men, whils thai had myght.
Bot sone all maistri gan thai mis.   superiority
God bring thaire saules untill his blis,
115 And God assoyl tham of thaire sin   absolve
   For the gude will that thai war in.   Amen.

Listens now, and leves me,   believe
   Who so lives thai sall se
That it mun be ful dere boght
120   That thir galay men have wroght.
Thai hoved still opon the flode
   And reved pouer men thaire gude: deprived
Thai robbed and did mekill schame,
   And ay bare Inglis men the blame.

125 Now Ihesus save all Ingland
       And blis it with his haly hand. Amen.

IV

    Edward oure cumly king
        In Braband has his woning,   dwelling
    With mani cumly knight;
        And in that land, trewly to tell,
5   Ordanis he still for to dwell,   determines
        To time he think to fight.

    Now God that es of mightes maste
        Grant him grace of the Haly Gaste
    His heritage to win.
10   And Mari moder of mercy fre,
    Save oure king and his menye
        Fro sorow and schame and syn.

    Thus in Braband has he bene,
        Whare he bifore was seldom sene,
15 For to prove thaire japes;   test
        Now no langer will he spare
    Bot unto Fraunce fast will he fare,
        To confort him with grapes.

    Furth he ferd into France;
20   God save him fro mischance,
    And all his cumpany.
        The nobill duc of Braband
    With him went into that land,
        Redy to lif or dy.

25 Than the riche floure de lice
  Wan thare ful litill prise;   glory
 Fast he fled for ferde.
  The right aire of that cuntre   heir
53v) Es cumen with all his knightes fre,
(a To schac him by the berd.

31 Sir Philip the Valayse,
  Wit his men in tho dayes,
 To batale had he thoght:
  He bad his men tham purvay, provide for
35 Withowten lenger delay,
  Bot he ne held it noght.

 He broght folk ful grete wone,   plenty
  Ay sevyn oganis one,
 That ful wele wapnid were: armed
40 Bot sone when he herd ascry
 That king Edward was nere tharby,
  Than durst he noght cum nere.

 In that mornig fell a mist,
  And when oure Inglis men it wist,
45 It changed all thaire chere
  Oure king unto God made his bone, prayer
 And God sent him gude confort sone,
  The weder wex ful clere.

 Oure king and his men held the felde
50 Stalwortly, with spere and schelde
 And thoght to win his right,
  With lordes and with knightes kene
 And other doghty men bydene,
  That war ful frek to fight.

55 When sir Philip of France herd tell
      That king Edward in feld walld dwell,
    Than gayned him no gle;   pleasure
      He traisted of no better bote,   expected
    Bot both on hors and on fote
60   He hasted him to fle.

    It semld he was ferd for strokes
      When he did fell his grete okes
    Obout his pavilyoune;
      Abated was than all his pride,
65 For langer thare durst he noght bide,
      His bost was broght all doune.

    The king of Beme had cares colde,
      That was ful hardy and ful bolde,
    A stede to umstride.
70   The king als of Naverne
    War faire feld in the ferene   hidden/bracken
      Thaire heviddes for to hide.

    And leves wele it es no lye,
      The felde hat Flemangrye
75 That king Edward was in,
      With princes that war stif ande bolde
(b) And dukes that war doghty tolde
      In batayle to bigin.

    The princes that war riche on raw
80   Gert nakers strike, and trumpes blaw.   drums
    And made mirth at thaire might:
      Both alblast and many a bow   crossbow
    War redy ralled opon a row,   ordered
      And ful frek for to fight.

85   Gladly thai gaf mete and drink
     So that thai suld the better swink   work
  The wight men that thar ware.
     Sir Philip of Fraunce fled for dout,
  And hied him hame with all his rout:
90   Coward, God giff him care.

  For thare than had the lely flowre
     Lorn all halely his honowre,   lost
  That so-gat fled for ferd: thus
     Bot oure king Edward come ful still,
95   When that he trowed no harm him till,
     And keped him in the berde.

V

  Lithes and the batail I sal bigyn
  Of Inglisch men & Normandes in the Swyn.

  Minot with mowth had menid to make
     Suth sawes & sad for sum mens sake;   true
  The wordes of sir Edward makes me to wake,
     Wald he salve us sone mi sorow suld slake;
5   War mi sorow slaked sune wald I sing:
     When God will sir Edward sal us bute bring.

  Sir Philip the Valas cast was in care;
     And said sir Hugh Kyret to Flandres suld fare,
  And have Normondes inogh to leve on his lare,   lesson
10   All Flandres to brin and mak it all bare;
  Bot, unkind coward, wo was him thare:
     When he sailed in the Swin it sowed him sare;   hurt
  Sare it tham smerted that ferd out of France;
     Thare lered Inglis men tham a new daunce.   taught

15 The burlase of Bruge ne war noght to blame;   citizens
    I pray Ihesu save tham fro sin and fro schame,
For thai war sone at the Sluse all by a name,
    Whare many of the Normandes tok mekill grame.   harm

    When Brug and Ipyre hereof herd tell,
20   Thai sent Edward to wit that was in Arwell;
Than had he no liking langer to dwell,
    He hasted him to the Swin with sergantes snell,   quick
To mete with the Normandes that fals were & fell,   cruel
    That had ment if thai might al Flandres to quell.

25 King Edward unto sail was ful sune dight   ready
    With erles and barons and many kene knight:
54r Thai come byfor Blankebergh on Saint Ions night;
(a)   That was to the Normondes a well sary sight.
    Yit trumped thai and daunced with torches ful bright,
30   In the wilde wanland was thaire hertes light.   waning

    Opon the morn efter, if I suth say,
    A meri man, Sir Robard out of Morlay,
At half-eb in the Swin soght he the way;
    Thare lered men the Normandes at bukler to play;
35 Helpid tham no prayer that thai might pray;
    The wreches er wonnen, thaire wapin is oway.   taken

    The Erle of Norhamton helpid at that nede,
    Als wise men of wordes and worthil in wede,
Sir Walter the Mawnay, God gif him mede,
    Was bold of body in batayl to bede.
40

    The duc of Lankaster was dight for to drive,   rush
    With mani mody man that thoght for to thrive,
Wele & stalworthy stint he that strive,   stopped
    That few of the Normandes left thai olive;

45   Fone left thai olive bot did tham to lepe;
      Men may find by the flod an C on hepe.

      Sir William of Klinton was eth for to knaw;   easy
        Mani stout bachilere broght he on raw.   line
      It semid with thaire schoting als it war snaw;
50   The bost of the Normandes broght thai ful law;
      Thaire bost was abated and thaire mekil pride,
(b)   Fer might thai noght fle bot thare bud tham bide.

      The gude Erle of Clowceter, God mote him glade,
      Broght many bold men with bowes ful brade;
55   To biker with the Normandes baldely thai bade   fight
      And in the middes the flode did tham to wade;
      To wade war tho wretches casten in the brim;   sea
      The kaitefs come out of France at lere tham to swim.

      I prays Iohn Badding als one of the best;
60   Faire come he sayland out of the suthwest,
      To prove of tha Normandes was he ful prest,   ready
      Till he had foghten his fill he had never rest.

      Iohn of Alle of the Sluys with scheltron ful schene
      Was comen into Cagent, cantly and kene,   keenly
65   Bote sone was his trumping turned to tene;   sorrow
      Of him had sir Edward his will als I wene.

      The schipmen of Ingland sailed ful swith
      That none of the Normandes fro tham might skrith; escape
      Who so kouth wele his craft thare might it kith: know
70   Of all the gude that thai gat gaf thai no tithe.

      Two hundreth and mo schippes on the sandes
      Had oure Inglis men won with thaire handes;

The kogges of Ingland war broght out of bandes   bonds
   And also the "Cristofir" that in the streme standes
75 In that stound thai stode, with stremers full still,
(b)   Til that thai wist full wele sir Edwards will.

Sir Edward, oure gude king wurthi in wall,
   Faght wele on that flude, faire mot him fall;
Als it es custom of king to confort tham all
80   So thanked he gudely the grete and the small,
He thanked tham gudely, God gif him mede,
   Thus come oure king in the Swin till that gude dede.

This was the batalle that fell in the Swin,
   Whare many Normandes made mekill din;
85 Wele war thai armed up to the chin;
   Bot God and sir Edward gert thaire bost blin,
Thus blinned thaire bost, als we wele ken;   ended
   God asoyle thaire sawles, sais all, Amen.

VI

Herkins how king Edward lay
With his men bifor Tournay.

Towrenay, yow has tight   determined
   To timber trey and tene   sorrow
A bore, with brenis bright   coats of mail
   Es broght opon yowre grene:
5 That es a semely sight,
   With schilterouns faire and schene:
Thi domes day es dight,
   Bot thou be war, I wene.

When all yowre wele is went
10   Yowre wo wakkins ful wide,   wakes

To sighing er ye sent
   With sorow on ilka syde:
Ful rewfull es yowre rent,   income
   All redles may ye ride;   without advice
15 The harmes that ye have hent   received
   Now may ye hele and hide.

Hides and hells als hende,
   For ye er cast in care;
Ful few find ye yowre frende
20   For all yowre frankis fare.   behaviour
Sir Philip sall yow schende,   ruin
   Whi leve ye at his lare?
No bowes now thar yow bende:
   Of blis ye er all bare.

25 All bare er ye of blis,
   No bost may be yowre bote,
All mirthes mun ye mis,
   Oure men sall with yow mote,   debate
Who sall yow clip and kys,   embrace
30   And fall yowre folk to fote:
A were is wroght, I wis,   war
   Yowre walles with to wrote   uproot

54v Wrote thai sall yowre dene,
(a)   Of dintes ye may yow dowt;
35 Yowre bigines sall men brene,   houses
   And breke yowre walles obout.
Ful redles may ye ren,
   With all yowre rewful rout;
With care men sall yow ken
40   Edward yowre lord to lout.   bow to

To lout yowre lord in land
   With list men sall yow lere;

Yowre harmes cumes at hand,
    As ye sall hastly here.
45 Now frendschip suld ye fande
    Of sir Philip yowre fere,   companion
To bring yow out of band,
    Or ye be broght on bere.   bier

On bere when ye er broght,
50   Than cumes Philip to late,
He hetes and haldes yow noght,   promises
    With hert ye may him hate.
A bare now has him soght
    Till Turnay the right gate,   way
55 That es ful wele bithoght
    To stop Philip the strate,   way
        Full still.
Philip was fain he moght
    Graunt sir Edward his will.

60 If ye will trow my tale,
    A duke tuke leve that tide,
A Braban brewd that bale,
    He bad no langer bide;
Giftes grete and smale
65   War sent him on his side;
Gold gert all that gale   injury
    And made him rapely ride   quickly
        Till dede;
In hert he was unhale;
70   He come thare moste for mede.

King Edward, frely fode,
    In Fraunce he will noght blin
To mak his famen wode   enemies
    That er wonand tharein   living
75 God that rest on rode
    For sake of Adams syn,

Strenklth him main & mode
His reght in France to win
And have.
80 God grante him graces gode,
And fro all sins us save. Amen.

VII

How Edward at Hogges unto land wan
And rade thurgh France or ever he blan.

(b) Men may rede in romance right
Of a grete clerk that Merlin hight;   was called
Ful many bokes er of him wreten,
Als thir clerkes wele may witten;
5 And yit in many prive nokes
May man find of Merlin bokes.
Merlin said thus with his mowth,
Out of the north into the sowth
Suld cum a bare over the se   boar
10 That suld mak many man to fle;
And in the se, he said ful right,
Suld he schew ful mekill might;   great
And in France he suld bigin
To mak tham wrath that er tharein;
15 Untill the se his taile reche sale
All folk of France to mekill bale.
Thus have I mater for to make,
For a nobill prince sake:
Help me, God, my wit es thin,
20 Now Laurence Minot will bigin.

A bore es broght on bankes bare
With ful batail bifor his brest;
For Iohn of France will he noght spare
In Normondy to tak his rest,
25 With princes that er proper and prest: prepared

- 43 -

Alweldand God of mightes maste,   Almighty
He be his beld, for he mai best,   help
Fader and Sun and Haly Caste.

Haly Caste, thou gif him grace,
30   That he in gude time may bigin,
And send to him both might & space
        His heritage wele for to win;
And sone asoyl him of his sin,
        Hende God, that herled hell.
35   For France now es he entred in
        And thare he dightes him for to dwell.   readies

He dwelled thare the suth to tell,
        Opon the coste of Normondy;
At Hogges fand he famen fell
        That war all full of felony:
40   To him thai makked grete maistri,
        And proved to ger the bare abyde;   force
Thurgh might of God & mild Mari
        The bare abated all thaire pride.

45   Mekill pride was thare in prese
        Both on pencell and on plate,   pennons/armour
When the bare rade, withouten rese,   haste
        Unto Cane the graythest gate.   straightest
55r Thare fand he folk bifor the gate
(a)   Thretty thowsand stif on stede:
51   Sir Iohn of France come al to late,
        The bare has gert thaire sides blede.

He gert tham blede if thai war bolde,
        For thare was slayne and wounded sore
55   Thretty thowsand, trewly tolde,
        Of pitalle war thare mekill more;   Infantry
Knightes was thare wele two score

That war new dubbed to that dance,
Helm and hevyd thai have forlore: *lost*
60   Than misliked Iohn of France.

More misliking was thare then,
    For fals treson alway thai wroght;
Bot, fro thai met with Inglismen,
    All thaire bargan dere thai boght.
65   Inglis men with site tham soght
    And hastily quit tham thaire hire;
And at the last forgat thai noght,
    The toun of Cane thai sett on fire.

That fire ful many folk gan fere,
70   When thai se brandes o ferrum flye;   *afar*
This have thai wonen of the were   *won*
    The fals folk of Normundy.
I sal yow lely how thai lye
    Dongen doun all in a daunce;   *dashed*
75   Thaire frendes may ful faire forthi
    Pleyn tham untill Iohn of France.   *complain*

Franche men put tham to pine   *trouble*
    At Cressy, when thai brak the brig;
That saw Edward with both his ine,   *eyes*
80   Than likid him no langer to lig.   *stay*
Ilk Inglis man on others rig   *back*
    Over that water er thai went;
To batail er thai baldly big,   *strong*
    With brade ax and with bowes bent.

85   With bent bowes thai war ful bolde
    For to fell of the Frankisch men;
Thai gert them lig with cares colde;
    Ful sari was sir Philip then.
He saw the toun oferrum bren,

90   And folk for ferd war fast fleand;
        The teres he lete ful rathly ren   quickly
           Out of his eghen, I understand.

        Than come Philip ful redy dight
           Toward the toun with al his rowt
95   With him come mani a kumly knight,
           And all umset the bare obout.   beset
(b) The bare made tham ful law to lout,
           And delt tham knokkes to thaire mede;
        He gert tham stumbill that war stout,
100   Thare helpid nowther staf ne stede.

        Stedes strong bilevid still   stayed
           Biside Cressy opon the grene;
        Sir Philip wanted all his will,
           That was wele on his sembland seen.   mien
105 With spere and scheld and helmis schene   bright
           The bare thai than durst thai noght habide:
        The king of Beme was cant and kene,
           Bot thare he left both play and pride.

        Pride in prese ne prais I noght
110   Omang thir princes prowd in pall;   robe
        Princes suld be wele bithoght,
           When kinges tham till counsaill call.
        If he be rightwis king, thai sall
           Maintene him both night and day,
115 els to lat his frendschip fall
           On faire manere, and fare oway.

        Oway es all thi wele, I wis,
           Franche man, with all thi fare;
        Of murnig may thou never mys,
120   For thou ert cumberd all in care:
        With speche ne moght thou never spare
           To speke of Ingliss men despite;

Now have thai made thi biging bare,   house
  Of all thi catell ertou quite.   deprived

125 Quite ertou that wele we knaw
  Of catell and of drewris dere   valuables
Tharfore lies thi hert ful law
  That are was blith als brid on brere.   before/bird
Inglis men sall yit to yere   this year
130 Knok thi palet or thou pas,   head
And mak the polled like a frere: shorn
  And yit es Ingland als it was.

Was thou nought, Franceis with thi wapin
  Bitwixen Cressy and Abuyle?
135 Whare thi felaws llen and gapin,
  For all thaire treget and thaire gile.   magic
Bisschoppes war thare in that while
  That songen all withouten stole:
Philip the Valas was a file,   coward
140 He fled and durst noght take his dole.   share

Men delid thare ful mani a dint
  Omang the gentill Genevayse;
Ful many man thaire lives tint   lost
  For luf of Philip the Valays.
55r Unkind he was and uncurtayse,
(a) I prais no thing his purviaunce   management
The best of France and of Artayse
  War al to dongyn in that daunce.

That daunce with treson was bygun
150 To trais the bare with sum fals gyn   betray
The Franche men said, "All es wun,
  Now es it tyme that we bigin,
For here es welth inogh to win,
  To make us riche for evermore."

155 Bot, thurgh thaire armure thik and thin
    Slaine thai war and wounded sore.

    Sore than sighed sir Philip;
      Now wist he never what him was best,
    For he es cast doun with a trip:
160   In Iohn of France es all his trest
    For he was his frend faithfulest,
      In him was full his affiance: trust
    Bot sir Edward wald never rest,
      Or thai war feld the best of France.

165 Of France was mekill wo, I wis,
      And in Paris tha high palays:
    Now had the bare with mekill blis
      Bigged him bifor Calais.
    Heres now how the romance sais
170   How sir Edward, oure king with croune,
    Held his sege bi nightes and dais
      With his men bifor Calays toune.

VIII

    How Edward als the romance sais
    Held his sege bifor Calais.

    Calays men, now mai ye care,
      And murnig mun ye have to mede;
    Mirth on mold get ye no mare;
      Sir Edward sall ken yow yowre crede.
5   Whilum war ye wight in wede   brave
      To robbing rathly for to run;
    Mend yow sone of yowre misdede;
      Yowre care es cumen, will ye it ken.

Kend it es how ye war kene
10   Al Inglis men with dole to dere;   sorrow
Thaire gudes toke ye al bidene,
    No man born wald ye forbere;
Ye spared noght with swerd ne spere
    To stik tham and thaire gudes to stele;
15 With wapin and with ded of were
    Thus have ye wonnen werldes wele.

Weleful men war ye, I wis,   successful
    Bot fer on fold sall ye noght fare;   earth
(b) A bare sal now abate yowre blis
20   And wirk yow bale on bankes bare;
He sall yow hunt als hund dose hare
    That in no hole sall ye yow hide;
For all yowre speche will he noght spare
    Bot bigges him right by yowre side.

25 Biside yow here the bare bigins
    To big his boure in winter tyde;   bower
And al bi tyme he takes his ines   houses
    With semly sergantes him biside.
The word of him walkes ful wide;
30   Ihesu save him fro mischance.
In batalil dar he wele habide
    Sir Philip and Sir Iohn of France.

The Franche men er fers and fell
    And mase grete dray when thai er dight;   disorder
35 Of tham men herd slike tales tell
    With Edward think thai for to fight,
Him for to hald out of his right
    And do him treson with thaire tales;
That was thaire purpos day and night
40   Bi counsall of the Cardinales.

Cardinales with hattes rede
   War fro Calays wele thre myle;
Thai toke thaire counsail in that stede
   How thai might sir Edward bigile.
45 Thai lended thare bote litill while
   Till Franche men to grante thaire grace;
Sir Philip was funden a file,
   He fled and faght noght in that place.

In that place the bare was blith,
50   For all was funden that he had soght:
Philip the Valas fled ful swith
   With the batail that he had broght.
For to have Calays had he thoght
   Al at his ledeing loud or still;   command
55 Bot al thaire wiles war for noght,
   Edward wan it at his will.

Lystens now and ye may lere,
   Als men the suth may understand,
The knightes that in Calais were
60   Come to sir Edward sare wepeand,
In kirtell one and swerd in hand
   And cried: "Sir Edward, thine are,
Do now, lord, bi law of land
   Thi will with us for evermare."

65 The nobill burgase and the best
   Come unto him to have thaire hire;
56r The comun puple war ful prest
(a)   Rapes to bring obout thaire swire: ropes/neck
Thai said all: "Sir Philip oure syre,
70   And his sun, sir Iohn of France,
Has left us ligand in the mire
   And broght us til this doleful dance.

Oure horses that were faire and fat
  Er etin up ilkone bidene;
75 Have we nowther conig ne cat   rabbit
  That thai ne er etin and hundes kene.
All er etin up ful clene,
  Es nowther levid biche ne whelp,
That es wele on oure sembland sene,
80   And thai er fled that suld us help."

A knight that was of grete renowne,
  Sir Iohn de Viene was his name,
He was wardaine of the toune,
  And had done Ingland mekill schame.
85 For all thaire boste thai er to blame,
  Ful stalworthly thare have thai strevyn;   fought
A bare es cumen to make tham tame,
  Kayes of the toun to him er gifen.

The kales er yolden him of the gate
90   Lat him now kepe tham if he kun;
To Calais cum thai all to late,
  Sir Philip and sir Iohn his sun.
Al war ful ferd that thare ware fun;
  Thaire leders may thai barely ban.   curse
All on this wise was Calais won;
  God save tham that it so-gat wan.

IX

  Sir David had of his men grete loss
  With sir Edward at the Nevil cross.

Sir David the Bruse   was at distance,
When Edward the Balloife   rade with his lance;
The north end of Ingland   teched him to daunce
When he was met on the more   with mekill mischaunce.

5   Sir Philip the Valayse may him noght avance;
     The flowres that faire war er fallen in Fraunce,
     The floures er now fallen that fers war and fell;
     A bare with his bataille has done tham to dwell.

(b) Sir David the Bruse said he suld fonde
     To ride thurgh all Ingland wald he noght wonde;
10   At the west minster hall suld his stedes stonde,
     Whils oure king Edward war out of the londe:
     Bot now has Sir David missed of his merkes
     And Philip the Valays with all thaire grete clerkes.

15   Sir Philip the Valais suth for to say,
     Sent unto sir David and faire gan him pray
     At ride thurgh Ingland thaire fomen to flay,   *scare*
     And said none es at home to let hym the way,   *hinder*
     None letes him the way to wend whore he will:
20   Bot with schipherd staves fand he his fill.

     Fro Philip the Valais was Sir David sent
     All Ingland to win fro Twede unto Trent;
     He broght mani berebag with bow redy bent;
     Thai robbed and thai reved and held that thai hent;
25   It was in the wanland that thai furth went;   *waning*
     For covaitise of catalle tho schrewes war schent;
     Schent war tho schrewes and ailed unsele   *unhappily*
     For at the Nevil cros nedes bud tham knele   *made*

     At the ersbisschop of York now will I bigyn,
30   For he may with his right hand assoyl us of sin:
     Both Dorem and Carlele thai wald never blin   *stop*
     The wirschip of Ingland with wappen to win;
56v Mekill wirschip thai wan and wele have thai waken,
(a) For syr David the Bruse was in that tyme taken.

35 When Sir David the Bruse satt on his stede,
    He said of all Ingland haved he no drede;
    Bot hende Iohn of Coupland a wight man in wede,
    Talked to David and kend him his crede.
    Thare was sir David so dughty in his dede,
40 The faire toure of Londen haved he to mede.

    Sone than was sir David broght unto the toure,
    And William the Dowglas with men of honowre;
    Ful swith redy servis fand thai thare a schowre,
    For first thai drank of the swete and sethin of the sowre.

45 Than sir David the Bruse makes his mone,
    The faire coroun of Scotland haves he forgone;
    He luked furth into France help had he none
    Of Philip the Valais ne yit of sir Iohn.

    The pride of sir David bigon fast to slaken;   lessen
50 For he wakkind the were that held him self waken;   woke
    For Philip the Valaise had he brede baken,
    And in the toure of Londen his ines er taken:
    To be both in a place thaire forward thai nomen,   took
    Bot Philip fayled thare and David es cumen.

55 Sir David the Bruse on this manere
    Said unto sir Philip al thir sawes thus sere: several
    "Philip the Valais thou made me be here,
(b) This es noght the forward we made are to yere: earlier
    Fals es thi forward and evyll mot thou fare,   agreement
60 For thou and sir Iohn thi son haves kast me in care."

    The Scottes with thaire falshede thus went thai obout
    For to win Ingland whils Edward was out.
    For Cuthbert of Dorem haved thai no dout;
    Tharfore at Nevel cros law gan thai lout,

65   Thare louted thai law and leved allane:
Thus was David the Bruse into the toure tane.

X

How king Edward and his menye
Met with the Spaniardes in the see.

I wald noght spare for to speke   wist I to spede,
Of wight men with wapin   and worthly in wede,
That now er driven to dale   and ded all thaire dede,   grave
Thai sall in the see gronde   fissches to fede;
5 Fele fissches thai fede   for all thaire grete fare,
It was in the wanland   that thai come thare.

Thai sailed furth in the Swin   in a somers tyde,
With trompes and taburns   and mekill other pride;   drums
The word of tho werkmen   walked full wide;
10 The gudes that thai robbed   in holl gan thai it hide;   hull
In holl than thai hided   grete welthes, als I wene,
Of gold and of silver   of skarlet and grene.

When thai sailed westward   tho wight men in were,
Thaire hurdis, thaire ankers hanged thai on here;   bulwarks
57r Wight men of the west   neghed tham nerr   approached
(a) And gert tham snaper in the snare   might thai no ferr, fall
Fer might thai noght flit   bot thare most thai fine,
And that thai bifore reved   than most thai tyne.   lose

Boy with thi blac berd   I rede that thou blin,
20 And sone set the to schrive   with sorow of thi sin;
If thou were on Ingland   noght saltou win,
Cum thou more on that coste   thi bale sall bigin: country

Thare kindels thi care kene men sall the kepe,
And do the dye on a day and domp in the depe.

25 Ye broght out of Bretayne yowre custom with care,
Ye met with the marchandes and made tham ful bare;
It es gude reson and right that ye evill misfare,
When ye wald in Ingland lere of a new lare,
New lare sall ye lere sir Edward to lout:
30 For when ye stode in yowre strenkith ye war all to stout.

XI

How gentill sir Edward with his grete engines
Wan with his wight men the castell of Gynes.

War this winter oway wele wald I wene
That somer suld schew him in schawes ful schene   thickets
Both the lely and the lipard suld geder on a grene.   lily
Mari, have mind of thi man thou whote wham I mene.
5 Lady, think what I mene I mak the my mone
Thou wreke gude king Edward on wikked syr Iohn.   avenge

Of Gynes ful gladly now will I bigin,
(b) We wote wele that woning was wikked for to win:
Crist that swelt on the rode for sake of mans sin,   cross
10 Hald tham in gude hele that now er tharein   health
Inglis men er tharein the kastell to kepe;
And Iohn of France es so wroth for wo will he wepe.

Gentill Iohn of Doncaster did a ful balde dede,
When he come toward Gines to ken tham thaire crede;
15 He stirt unto the castell withowten any stede;
Of folk that he fand thare haved he no drede,

Dred in hert had he none of all he fand thare:
Faine war thai to fle for all thaire grete fare.

A letherin ledderr and a lang line,   leather ladder
20 A small bote was tharby that put tham fro pine;   boat
The folk that thai fand thare was faine for to fyne; submit
Sone thaire diner was dight and thare wald thai dine
Thare was thaire purpose to dine and to dwell,
For treson of the Franche men that fals war and fell.

25 Say now, sir Iohn of France how saltou fare?
That both Calays and Cynes has kindeld thi care;
If thou be man of mekil might lepe up on thi mare,
Take thi gate unto Cines and grete tham wele thare,
Thare gretes thi gestes and wendes with wo:
30 King Edward has wonen the kastell tham fro.

Ye men of Saint Omers trus ye this tide,
57v And puttes out yowre pavillownes with yowre mekill pride;
(a) Sendes efter sir Iohn of Fraunce to stand by yowre syde,
A bore is boun yow to biker that wele dar habyde,
35 Wele dar he habide batalle to bede,
And of yowre sir Iohn of Fraunce haves he no drede.

God save sir Edward his right in ever ilka nede,
And he that will noght so evil mot he spede;
And len oure sir Edward his life wele to lede,
40 That he may at his ending have hevin till his mede.

A—M—E—N.

Notes

N.B. References are to lines in individual poems.

Any editor of Minot is unlikely to improve on the extensive list of phrases given by Hall or the painstaking work on metre by Collette. The latter field is not within the scope of this edition but in the former case we include a representative selection of phrases culled from romance in order to show the reader just how deeply Minot's vocabulary had been penetrated by the genre. We have also elected not to record every emendation of every previous editor. Both Hall and Stedman do this but as the text of Minot is virtually problem free and emendations are frequently trivial we have decided to preserve as many of the ms. readings as we can in our text and to make and record only such emendations as are necessary to correct obvious scribal error. Throughout our text the runic characters 'thorn' and 'yogh' have been represented by 'th' and 'y'.

The sources for the historical notes and biographical details are listed in the bibliography. Facts have been checked in works published since Hall's editions, in particular for the Anglo-French war and politics in the appropriate Oxford History of England (McKisack 1959), in Prestwich (1980) and Perroy (1951) and for Scotland in Grant (1984). Where these authorities have no information or have disagreed, reference has been sought elsewhere and further works are cited in the bibliography.

Poem I

1-8. The opening stanza contains much that is reminiscent of the Middle English romance both in its formulaic diction and its invocatory nature. The device of linking stanzas by the repetition of a word in the last line of the succeeding one is

to be found in the *Awntyrs of Arthure at the Tarne Wathelyn.*
The formula 'in trone' may be found in *Havelok the Dane*: 'Iesu
Crists...that sittes in trone' (line 1316), Erl of Toulous: 'God,
that syttyth in trone.' (line 461), and *Emare*: 'Jesu that is
kyng in trone.' (line 1). For 'bote of all my bale' compare *Sir
Amadace*: 'God that is bote of all bale.' (line 202). It is also
common for the invocation to God to include some mention of
his attributes as a creator of the earth and the universe
compare *Emare*: 'As thou shoope bothe sonne and mone' (line 2),
Sir Isumbras: 'God that made both erthe and hevenne / And all
this worlde in deyes seven' (lines 1-2).

12. Edward III (b. 1312, r. 1327-77), married Philippa of
Hainault a niece of Philip VI of France in 1328. Edward was a
nephew of the last Capetian king, Charles IV (r. 1322-28), and
had a claim to the throne of France through his mother,
Isabella (see genealogy p. 25). Salic law was invoked in 1328
to bar inheritance through the female line. The turmoil in
England following the deposition of Edward II in 1327 meant
that the English were in no position to press a claim
effectively, and Edward III did simple homage to Philip VI (see
l. 45) at Amiens in 1329 for lands in France (see above p. 21).

19-21. 'Ilka side...noght at hide', both these phrases are of
residual meaning and are not unusual as metrical padding in
romance. See *Ywain and Gawain*: 'In chambers high, es noght at
hide, / And in solers on ilka side' (lines 807-8), a text also
in Cotton Galba E. ix. (see Appendix 3).

42. John Randolph became Earl of Moray in 1332 on the death of
his father, Thomas. He avenged the defeat of the Scots by
Edward Balliol (see line 72 and Poem IX, line 2 and note) at
Dupplin Moor (1332) by driving Balliol, a claimant to the
Scottish throne, out of Scotland. Earl John was killed at
Neville's Cross in 1346.

45. Philip VI (r. 1328-50), a cousin of Charles IV and Isabella,
was chosen king of France in 1328. His claim was through the
male line and in addition he was already an experienced
administrator (see genealogy p. 25).

60. 'wild...tame', these epithets refer respectively to the Gaelic speaking Highlanders and the English speaking Lowlanders.

71. Compare *Sege of Melayne*: 'And liste nothynge of playe.' (line 1252).

72. John Comyn of Badenoch was nephew of John Balliol, absentee king of Scotland. In 1306 Robert I (the Bruce, r. 1306-29) murdered Comyn thereby ousting the Balliol/Comyn faction, and seized the throne.

Poem II

Title 'the' not in ms.

10. Compare *Sege of Melayne*: 'Or he will kindill cares full calde.' (line 597).

11. Compare *Erl of Toulous*: 'Was crakkyde many a crowne.'(line 72).

19. 'Rughfute riveling', this is the distinctive coarse boot of raw hide which was worn by the Scots.

22. 'Brug', ms.'brig.'

25. 'Skotte...Burghes', ms. 'skottes...burghes.'

Poem III

1-10. Again, this is an opening which would not be out of place in a romance. See note to Poem I, lines 1-8 above.

11. 'trewly', ms. 'trely.'

13. Lewis of Bavaria (r. 1314-46), Holy Roman Emperor, married a sister of Philippa of Hainault. He was implacably opposed by

pope John XXII (r. 1316-34), and later — for different reasons — by Clement VI (r. 1342-52). Lewis supported the English at first in the war with France, making Edward III an honorary Vicar-General of the Empire in 1338 for lands to the west of Cologne. The emperor was paid the huge sum of £60,000, (equivalent to the entire income of the English Exchequer in 1324), but did little. He was allied to Philip VI from 1341.

25. John III, Duke of Brabant (d. 1355), joined Edward III also in return for £60,000 and the promise of the establishment of the wool staple at Antwerp. John III also did little. Minot's interpretation of this piece of diplomacy is somewhat over enthusiastic.

68. 'knokked', ms. 'knoked.'

75. The 'Cristofer' was captured by the French, but whether from Sluys, Middelburgh or Yarmouth (Isle of Wight), is uncertain, as is the date on which the vessel was taken.

75-80. 'galayes...tarettes...gallotes', The galley was a large ship propelled by rowers, the gallot a smaller version of the same. The taret was also large and like a galley but was primarily a transport. A cog (see Poem VI, line 73), was a broad, deep ship (see Hall 1914, p. 53).

77. 'went', ms. 'wen.'

102. This is a common romance tag, see Northern *Octavian*: 'Both yn yron and yn stele.' (line 824)

109. Compare *Ywain and Gawain*: 'Thare I fand the fayrest thorne / That ever groued sen God was born' (lines 353-4).

117. This is a call to attention typical of romance and, as Hall rightly points out, usually found at a moment of division in the narrative. It may, therefore, seem rather surprising that it comes here at the end of a lyric. However, taking the poems as a whole, the call makes perfect sense for in Poem IV Edward will get his revenge. Indeed, in the ms. Poems III and IV are

written continuously but in different forms and we are attracted by Hall's suggestion that this call was an addition made by Minot in the revision of his work.

125. 'Ihesus', ms. 'Ihc' with a mark of abbreviation above the 'c' which may perhaps signify that the correct reading should be 'Ihesus Crist.'

Poem IV

7. 'of mightes maste', compare *Sege of Melayne* 'Art thou noghte halden of myghtis maste.' (line 551).

15. 'prove', ms. 'pue'. Stedman suggests that the ms. gives no mark of abbreviation here, but the appropriate symbol is perfectly clear.

25. 'de lice', ms. 'delice'.

37. 'broght', ms. 'bcoght'.

45. Compare *Sir Launfal*, 'That doth my changy chere.' (line 921). In *Sir Gawain and the Greene Knight* the following examples occur: 'His cher ful oft con chaunge' and 'And often chaunged his cher' (711 & 2169) though in both of these cases the phrase may mean 'changed direction.' In ms. 'changed' appears as 'shanged.'

55. 'sir' written above the line in ms.

58-59. Compare *Octavian* 'Florent sawe none odur bote / But that he must fyght on fote.' (lines 1321-2)

61. The chronicler Murimuth claimed that Philip VI chopped down trees and broke down bridges to prevent Edward III following. See Appendix 2, II 'An Invective.'

67. John the Blind, King of Bohemia (r. 1310-1346) was instrumental in persuading Lewis of Bavaria to break with Edward III. King John was killed at the battle of Crecy.

68. 'ful', ms. 'fur'.

70. Philip of Evreux and Navarre (r. 1328-43), father of Charles 'the Bad' king of Navarre (b. 1332, r. 1343-87). Philip married Jeanne (see genealogy p. 25) otherwise Joan, daughter of Louis X (r. 1314-16), elder brother of Philip V (r. 1316-22), Charles IV and Isabella. It is significant therefore that had Charles of Navarre been alive in 1328, he would have had a similar claim to the throne of France to Edward III – although Salic law had already been adduced in 1316 to bar his mother Joan from the throne (i.e. to bar female succession). In 1328 the possibility that Joan might bear male children was very much at issue in addition to Edward's claim. Philip V was hoist by his own petard in 1322 when he left no male heir other than his brother Charles IV. As Charles of Navarre put it in 1358 'my mother would have been king of France if she had been a man.' Charles at first supported Edward III, but later campaigned on his own account for a time , although in 1370 he was still making diplomatic overtures to Edward.

71. This line is the most difficult in the entire corpus of Minot's verse. Hall correctly points out that in the ms. the words 'feld in the' are "in smaller writing than the other words, as if they had been inserted afterwards." He suggests the emendation: 'War fain for fered in the ferene." Scholle suggests 'felld' i.e. 'hid'. Stedman gives 'War faire fayne in the ferene.' Our own feeling is that Skeat's notion that 'feld' is an error for 'fled' has much merit and is certainly the simplest solution.

Poem V

Title: Sluys (now Vlissingen) is sited at the mouth of the Swyn (Zwin).

NOTES

1. 'Minot with mowth', Minot here names himself for the first time. It is the phrase 'with mowth' that gives us confidence in the idea of Minot as author rather than recorder or scribe (though, of course, he may have been a scribe or secretary). Compare the ending of *Sir Launfal*:

> Thomas Chestre made thys tale
> Of the noble knyght Syr Launfale,
>   Good of chyvalrye;
> Ihesus, that ys Hevene-kyng,
>   Yeve us alle blessyng,
> And Hys Modyr Marye! AMEN.

Here another elusive medieval poet introduces himself though there is also the nagging doubt that this may be a scribal 'signature'. See also Ywain and Gawain : 'It es no llfand man with mowth / That half hir cumforth tel kowth.' (lines 1381–2).

8. Hugues Quirlet, Admiral of France, died of wounds received at Sluys in 1340.

23. 'Normandes', ms. 'Nomandes'.

27. 24 June.

32. Robert, Lord Morley (d. 1360), Admiral of the northern fleet, fought at Crecy, Calais and Winchelsea.

36. 'er', ms. 'es'.

37. William de Bohun (d. 1360), a great friend and adviser of Edward III was made first Earl of Northampton in 1337. A successful campaigner in Brittany, he fought at Crecy and captured the King of Majorca.

38. 'worthli in wede', another common alliterative phrase. Compare Sege of Melayne (line 867), *Sir Gawain and the Greene Knight* (line 135), *Sir Degare* (line 1892), *Morte Arthure* (line 2709).

39. Walter de Mauny (d. 1372) was a Hainaulter who came to England with Queen Philippa. A successful commander on land and at sea, Mauny led the raid on Cadsand in 1337, fought in Brittany, at Calais and at Winchelsea. He was elevated to the peerage by Edward III.

40. Stedman inserts 'barn' after 'body'; Scholle 'man'. Hall sugests 'burne' but the line seems to us to be acceptable as it stands.

41. Henry of Grosmont (b. 1310, d. 1361), Earl of Derby 1337, Earl of Lancaster 1345, Duke of Lancaster 1351. Fought at Cadsand 1337, Flamengerie 1339, Winchelsea 1350 and in the 1359-60 campaign in France. John of Gaunt (d. 1399) married Blanche, Grosmont's daughter and heiress, and inherited his lands and titles. Grosmont's *Livre de Seyntz Medicines*, a personal account of the author's encounters with the seven deadly sins, is a rare survival. For a full account of Henry of Grosmont see Fowler (1969).

47. William Clinton (d. 1354), Earl of Huntingdon 1337, had supported Edward III against Mortimer at Nottingham in 1330, fought at Halidon Hill and at Crecy. He was much involved in diplomatic activity.

53. Hugh Audley (d. 1347), Earl of Gloucester 1337, had fought in Scotland in 1335 and was at Flamengerie.

59. John Badding. Unidentified.

63. Jan van Eyle of Sluys. Captain of the 'Cristofer' after it was captured from the English. When the 'Cristofer' was repossessed by the English, van Eyle was in turn captured and despite an offer of ransom was beheaded.

84. 'Normandes', ms. 'Nomandes'.

NOTES

Poem VI

41. 'yowre', ms. 'yow.'

62. 'brewd' so Scholle and Stedman, ms. 'brwed.'

74. 'tharein', ms., 'thare in.'

77. Compare *Ywain and Gawain*: 'I wil hir luf with main and mode.' (line 1031).

Poem VII

Title 'Thurgh', ms. 'Tiurgh'.

1. At this point Minot is particularly close to the ethos and the idiom of Middle English romance and it is not uncommon to find romances alluding to their sources (or themselves?) in this manner. Of course, in this context the phrase may well denote 'French.'

2. It may be no coincidence that the *Prophecies of Merlin* appear on ff. 49r-50v of Cotton Galba E. ix., only two leaves before the poems of Minot (see Appendix 3). Hall prints the text on pp. 101-109 of his 1887 edition.

23. John of France (b. 1319, r. 1350-64), Duke of Normandy 1331, was besieging the strategically important fortress of Aiguillon (Guienne) in 1346, but abandoned the siege to assist in hunting down Edward III's expeditionary force and marched north arriving, however, too late to avert the French defeat at Crecy. He was captured at Poitiers in 1356, was released in 1360, but returned to captivity in 1363 and died in captivity in 1364.

53. 'tham', not in ms. but adopted by Hall and Stedman.

58. 'daunce', as Hall points out this is one of Minot's favourite ironic usages.

61. 'misliking', ms. 'misliling.'

82. Jean de Vienne (d. 1351) had served in Brittany with John Duke of Normandy in 1341.

91. Compare *Emare*: 'And he hyt redde, Y unthurstonde: / The teres downe gan he lete.' (lines 548-9).

112. 'till', ms. 'toll.'

148. 'al todongyn', ms. 'alto dongyn.'

Poem VIII

11. 'al bidene', ms. 'albidene.'

28. 'sergantes', ms. 'segantes.'

62. 'are': this is the ms. reading though all editors add 'we' before it. Hall admits that the 'ms. is perhaps right.' We think it is and that 'are' derives from Old English 'ar' (mercy). Compare *Havelok the Dane*: 'And seyden, 'Levedi, Kristes ore and youres' (line 2797) and more similar still *Octavian*: 'The Crysten prysoners were full fayne, / When the Sarsyns were y-slayne, / And cryed, 'Lord, thyn ore!' (lines 1681-3)

96. 'so-gat', ms. 'so gat.'

Poem IX

1. David II (b. 1324, r. 1329-71), son of Robert I. David Bruce was sent to France for safe-keeping from 1334-41, was captured at Neville's Cross (1346) and was in captivity until 1357 when he was ransomed. The ransom was still partly unpaid on his death in 1371.

NOTES

2. John Balliol (see I, line. 42) , father of Edward Balliol mentioned here, , was selected as king of Scotland in 1292. Until they captured David Bruce in 1346, the English supported the Balliols.

25. 'in the wanland' i.e. at the time of the waning moon.

29. William de la Zouche, keeper of the privy seal 1335-37, treasurer of England 1337-40, was Archbishop of York from 1342-52.

37. John of Coupland was made for life by the capture of David Bruce. Coupland was a royal pensioner with £500 a year from 1347 and in the same year was made constable of Roxburgh Castle. He was sheriff of Northumberland from 1350-54 and was assassinated in 1364.

37. 'hende', ms. 'hinde.'

42. William Douglas of Liddesdale, also captured at Neville's Cross, has been described as 'violent and ambitious.' He was murdered by his godson William Douglas in 1353, which greatly increased Scotland's political stability.

44. 'sethin', ms. 'sevin' or 'senin.'

63. St. Cuthbert (d. 687).

Poem X

19. 'thou', ms. 'tho'. Blackbeard was a Genoese naval commander at Sluys. He offered to fight for England, but was rejected. He defeated the Earl of Pembroke at La Rochelle in 1372.

30. 'all to', ms. 'allto.'

Poem XI

13. John of Doncaster is usually cited in support of Yorkshire connections for Minot, who, it is postulated, singles out Doncaster for praise as a Yorkshireman. While Doncaster's Yorkshire origin is likely, he is described elsewhere as an archer of Calais. In any case he seems to have been an adventurer who sold Guines to Edward III after it was captured.

15. 'withowten', ms. 'with owten.'

34. Compare *Sege of Melayne*: 'That ever to bekyre es bayne' (line 186)

36. 'have', ms. 'haveves.'

Appendix 1

The Vows of the Heron

Thomas Wright (1859, p. 1 note) observed that the dialect of 'The Vows of the Heron' is strongly northern French and probably that of Artois, the county claimed by the central figure of the poem, Robert of Artois. More recent work suggests that the dialect is Picard (Whiting, 1945). It is certainly dated before the death of Robert in the Breton campaign of 1342-3 and probably dates to 1340 or just after, Wright suggests, on the evidence of an allusion to the captivity of the Earl of Suffolk in that year (1859, lines 202ff and notes).

Lewis (1968) refers to a long succession of French propagandists who list Robert of Artois amongst those who weakened France from within. Froissart certainly saw Robert of Artois' defection to England as a major cause of the Hundred Years War. The harbouring of a vassal (Robert), by another vassal (Edward) in defiance of the overlord (Philip VI) added a feudal dimension to the dynastic disputes brought about by Edward's exclusion from the succession in 1328. The sheltering of Robert of Artois by Edward was the principal reason given by Philip VI for confiscating Gascony from Edward III in May 1337, thus setting off the war.

There is much in the poem which is reminiscent of Froissart and his contemporary source, Jean le Bel. The lack of historicity ties the accounts together: the only date given in 'The Vows of the Heron', for example, is apparently inaccurate. However, like Froissart the poem has much to tell us about personal attitudes and intentions, about chivalry and the conduct of war, and certain of the vows 'miraculously' come true, and are later recorded by Froissart !

A close examination of the poem and its precursor has a different tale to tell. Whiting (1945), Taylor (1987) and the analysis carried out for this edition all contribute to a view that 'The Vows of the Heron' is not a 'gentle fiction' describing a chivalric feast, but a clear indictment of English war policy and a fierce satire on Edward III and his courtiers. The precursor was 'The Vows of the Peacock', written c. 1310 in which Edward II and his courtiers vow destruction against Robert Bruce. Those alive in 1340 would be all too aware of the outcome of those vows, at Bannockburn in 1314.

Close scrutiny of 'The Vows of the Heron' shows certain of the vows and the circumstances in which they were made to have been absurd. For example the Earl of Derby's daughter who is 'greatly in love' with the Earl of Salisbury was only seven years old at most. The earl, whose eye she closes, was already blind in one eye. Walter de Mauny's proposed raid on a town of Sir Godemar de Fay was probably a fiasco and so on. The queen's vow not to have her baby until hostilities were under weigh was recognised by Wright as being 'coarse.' Further details of those mentioned in the poem, and their vows, are given in notes following the text of the poem.

Taylor's view (1987, pp. 238-9) that 'The Vows of the Heron' is 'one of the most remarkable and perplexing political poems of the fourteenth century' is certainly true, and the publication here of a text in English allows the reader to decide whether it is an attack on English war policy perhaps launched by people suffering in the Low Countries, or whether it is 'anti-war propaganda.'

This prose translation is closely based on that of Wright (1859) and differs only in points of detail and general modernisation of idiom.

The Vows of the Heron

In the month of September, when summer is in decline, when the pretty little birds have lost their song, and the vines dry up, and the grapes are ripe, and the trees shed their leaves and they cover the roads, in the year 1338[1], as I assure you, Edward was in London in his marble palace; with him sat dukes, earls and courtiers, and ladies, and girls, and many other women. His neighbours call him Edward Louis. The King sat at table not thinking any harm: in thoughts of love he was looking downwards. He was called cousin of the noble King of France and he held him in affection as his loyal neighbour: he planned neither battle nor strife against him. But I suppose that when Fortune turns, the words soon arise from which he will have great bitterness.

So it transpired at this particular time through a noble vassal of great lineage. He was named Robert of Artois as the courtiers say: he started the war and the horrible strife through which many a good knight was thrown down dead, many a lady was made a widow and many a child made a poor orphan, many a good sailor met his end and many an honest woman put to different fates, and many a beautiful church burned and ruined: and this will happen again if Jesus does not put a stop to it.

Lords, at that time of which I am telling you, when the air cools after the warm weather and nature falls from its joy and the leaves fall in the woods and the meadows lose their flowers, Edward was in London and his nobles with him: there was a great assembly of the people of his country. There was Robert of Artois,[2] a man of great nobility. He was banished from the noble country of France, driven from the land of King Philip the clear-faced,[3] and did not dare to stay in the country on this side of the sea: neither in Flanders, nor Namur, nor in Auvergne. Furthermore, he was deserted by all, both family and friends, for love of the good king who held St Denis, the King of England excepted by whom he was well-received. He protected Robert against his enemies and held him in great affection because he was his friend, of the same lineage on the side of the fleur-de-lis.

That day the noble earl Robert was in London and he was seized by the desire to go hunting because he remembered the very noble and praised land of France from which he was banished. That day he went fowling over fields and over heaths: he carries a little falcon which he had bred - they call it a muskadin falcon in that country. He went fowling along the river until he had caught a heron. As soon as he caught it his face reddened and he says that he will give it to Edward Louis and make those of his country take vows upon it. Off he goes to London and his dependents with him, he went into the kitchen and there the heron was put. There it was very well plucked and stuffed and was roasted as is usual.

The heron was placed between two silver dishes and Count Robert took two players on the viol and a giterne player to accompany them. He called two girls, daughters of two nobles: they carried the heron into the vaulted palace. The two girls sing also as if for pleasure and Robert cries out loud with loud cries: "Open the ranks, open, wicked and sordid people! Let through the nobles who have been seized by love. Here is food for the gentry, for those who are dependents, for the loving ladies who have bright faces. Lords, I have a heron which my falcon has taken and here I don't think that there is any coward at table except the noble lovers who are adorned with love. I have taken what I think to be the most cowardly bird of all: let everyone be sure of this. For the heron is always thus by nature - as soon as it sees its shadow it is all astounded: it cries and brays as if it were being murdered. The people of this country ought to make their vows on it, and since it is a coward, I say as my opinion, I will give it to the greatest coward who is, or ever was, alive: that is Edward Louis, disinherited from the noble country of France of which he is the rightful heir. But his heart has failed him and for his cowardice he will die deprived of it. So he must vow on the heron what he thinks."

And when the king hears this his face becomes all reddened, his heart chafes with anger and spite and he says: "Since 'coward' is thrown in my face, it is right that I be worth more and I will tell my thoughts and the deed will be seen if I live long or I shall die in the attempt to accomplish my vow. I vow and promise to God of Paradise, and to his sweet mother by whom he was nursed, that before the year is passed or completed I will defy the king of St Denis and I will cross the sea, my subjects with me, and right through Hainault I will pass Cambresis and I will stay at my will in Vermandois, and fire will be set through the whole country, and there I will await my mortal enemies - that is Philip of Valois who bears the fleur-de-lis - until one full month has passed. And if he comes against me, and his subjects with him, I will fight him - let him be sure of that - if I had only one man against ten.[4] Does he think, then, that he can rob me of my lands and country? If I did homage to him - at which I am amazed - I was young so it is not worth two ears of corn.[5] I swear as king, by St George and St Denis, that since the time of Hector, Achilles or Paris, or of King Alexander who conquered many countries,[6] no such truce was made in France by bachelor or noble which I intend to make before the year forty-six if he does not come to meet me with his subjects. But I renounce him, whether in castles or fiefs, for I will make war on him in both word and deed. With my oath I have undertaken this vow."

When Robert hears him he gave way to a smile and said in a whisper: "Now I have my will since through the heron which I caught today a great war will begin as I want. I ought to be pleased, by God of Paradise, for I was wrongfully separated and parted from the good king, and I was banished from the noble country of France and divorced with grief from all my good friends. Furthermore, he was my brother-in-law yet he has taken my wife, my daughter and my children and put them in his prison. But, by the faith which I owe to my daughter and sons, I will live in France before I die, if it please Jesus Christ, for I have friends there. I am descended from monseigneur St Louis and there I shall see Philip who cries 'St Denis - Montjoie!' Be sure that I was a privy councillor to the King of France, who is very powerful, at the time when he was established regent, and on all occasions I advised him loyally for which I have only been paid a bad reward. But, by that God who was put on the cross and struck by the spear of the knight Longis, I will go to France - I am not at all frightened - and I will fight before I leave it. Now whatever happens I have undertaken it thus and if I live long my vow is accomplished."

When Robert of Artois had made his vow he took the two dishes - which were solid silver - and the heron in them and made a present to the king. The two minstrels play their viols sweetly and the they harmonise sweetly with the giterne player and nearby the two girls sing prettily: "I go to the green countryside for love teaches me to do so." There you could see very joyfully great pleasure in game and solace which after that day turned to great disaster and will still unless God takes pity on it.

And Robert of Artois did not stay there; he jumped over the table quite openly and quickly. He went first to the Earl of Salisbury[7] who sits near his mistress who is greatly in love - she was the Earl of Derby's daughter[8] who loved him loyally and was gentle, courtly and of beautiful bearing. And Robert said to him, very gracefully: "Fair sir, you who are full of great boldness: in the name of Jesus Christ to whom the world belongs, make a vow of true devotion to our heron without any delay I humbly pray you."

He replied to Robert: "And why and how could I chance my body so highly that I might completely accomplish any vow ? For I serve the lady who is chief in beauty and as love teaches me: If the Virgin Mary were present and deity were to be taken from her I should not be able to tell between the two. I have asked her for love but she refuses but gracious hope gives me to understand that I shall yet have mercy if I live long. So I pray the lady, devoutly from my heart, that she lends me a finger of her hand and puts it entirely over my right eye."

"By my faith," said the lady, "the woman who requires to have the full strength of her lover's body would act basely if she refused to touch him with one finger: and so I am ready to lend him two."

Immediately she placed two fingers on his right eye and thus she closed his eye and shut it up firmly. And he asked her very gracefully: "Lady, is it quite closed?" "Yes, certainly." Then he spoke his deepest thought aloud: "I vow and swear to God Almighty and to his sweet mother resplendent with beauty, that it shall never be opened, for wind or weather, for hurt or torture, or for disaster till I am in France where there are good people. And I shall have set fire everywhere, and I shall have fought with great force against the bold Philip's men. If, by good will, I am not taken in battle I will hold Edward to accomplish his plan. Now let anything happen for there is no alternative." Then the lady removed her finger and the people saw that the eye stayed shut and when Robert hears it he is filled with great joy.

When the Earl of Salisbury had made his vow (and the eye always stayed shut in the war) the noble Robert of Artois did not stay idle. He appealed to the lady, the Earl of Derby's daughter: "Lady," he said, "In the name of Jesus Christ, now vow the rights of this country on the heron." "As you will, sir," said the lady, "for I vow and promise to God of Paradise that I will not marry for any man alive, for duke, earl or sovereign prince, or marquis, before this servant has completely accomplished the vow which he has so loftily undertaken for my love; and when he returns, if he escapes alive, I give him my body, gladly and forever." When the servant heard this he was overcome and his heart was gladder and braver for it.

When the noble woman had expressed her thought of serving her friend, for so it pleased her Count Robert of Artois did not delay. He took again the dishes of silver (the bearer gave them up), for he was much exercised in heart and mind to say such words as should bring grief to France because he had lost the noble country which is so rich and he was much grieved at this. He spoke his mind to Walter de Mauny:[9] "Sir," said Robert, "if it pleases you, vow your honourable pleasure to our heron." Walter replies: "I ought to be silent. I do not know how to make a vow which can be achieved but as I see here a company that is honourable I will make a effort to guard my own honour. Therefore, I vow and promise to the honoured Virgin who bore God who made the heaven and the dew, that one morning I shall set fire to a good town fortified with towers, inclosed with marshes, and surrounded with strongpoints: Godemar de Fay has long held it. This town shall be ruined by me and the people slain and lie with their mouths gaping and I shall go away from it that same day all sound and rejoicing without a wound in my flesh nor my people's who entered with me. Now may God give me power to turn my thought into action!" When Robert hears him he is very pleased and says: "The thing is hard if it were done thus and many a good man will die before it is accomplished."

When Walter de Mauny had made his vow, Robert of Artois, of whom I have spoken before, has taken the two dishes up again and has raised them. The three minstrels have struck their strings and the two girls have sung aloud: "Loyal loves lead us which have enchanted us." The count has called upon the noble Earl of Derby[10] and prays him for the sake of God and the Trinity, that he vows his will and pleasure to the heron. The earl replied with great humility: "Robert, I will do it at your wish and I vow and promise and it shall be achieved that when the English king has led us over there into the land of France

of which so much has been said that I shall seek a powerful
and redoubtable count until I have found him and demand jousts
of him, if he has the heart to dare it. I mean Louis of
Flanders[11] - so the people of Philip the strong-limbed of
Valois call him, Philip who makes himself King of France
against the will of good King Edward who has so much pride. As
St Thomas have me I have vowed in my heart and if he does not
meet me with very great power, by the faith which I owe to
Edward the strong-limbed I shall have set the fire so near him
that it shall be clearly seen and looked at by him. Now
whatever happens I have vowed it." When Robert hears it he is
greatly pleased and says: "War thus made will be friendship to
me, the time will yet come, if God intends it, that my children
will be let out of prison and I shall perhaps be able to hurt
those who have hurt me."

When Robert of Artois had said his piece he took the two
dishes again and raised them up. He came to the Earl of
Suffolk[12] and said to him; "Fair sir, you who are English over
there, vow to our heron and God will help you." The earl
replied: "I will not fail you for I vow and promise, and my
body shall keep to it, that if the English king leads us over
there into France where there are many knights, that truly my
body shall pursue the son of an emperor who possesses much
goodness. I mean the King of Bohemia.[13] I do not know if he
will come there but if I meet him, by God, he shall have battle
with me without fail, my body has desired it, either with
glaive or sword so that he shall feel it. He shall be thrown
clean to the ground and I will have his horse: I do not know if
he will give it me. Now whatever happens just so will it be."

When John of Beaumont[14] heard this he sighed very deeply -
know for certain it annoyed him very much - and said: "Your
heart has vowed outrageous vows. I am kinsman to the good
king who has conquered so much in great nobleness and will do
so still. Though he hates me and is over there I love him and
will not fail him when he is in need. By the Lord who created
the world, who was born of the Virgin when the star rose, I

will cause you to be taken - I will not let you down - the powerful King of Bohemia will hold you in prison and it will not turn out otherwise whoever objects."[15]

The Earl of Suffolk said: "Now let it be so without anger. Love, courage, and the great desire we have to challenge the land of France causes us to seek and desire the great task. These lovers must be exerting themselves for love, for he who loves by love must advance himself. One ought to labour in word and deed, everyone will do well when he comes to the approach but the hardest will be to return back."

Count Robert of Artois did not delay there, he makes the minstrels work on the viol and these ladies dance to prepare the prey. He takes the two dishes and the heron again and begins to talk to Jean de Faukemont:[16] "And you, sir, who make yourself much feared in war: now vow to the heron the right to adventure." And he replied: "I ought not to meddle with a vow for I have nothing to give. I am a poor man and not desirous of sharing in it. But for the love of you, and to keep my honours, I vow and promise and give assurance of it that if the English king passed beyond the sea and entered France through Cambresis, I would go and set fire before him and I would spare neither church nor altar, neither pregnant woman nor infant, nor kinsman nor friend however much he should love me as long as he should wish to grieve King Edward. To accomplish this vow I would pain my body. Now whatever happens I will take on the adventure." And one said to another: "Such a man is to be loved who would increase and raise the honour of his lord."

Count Robert of Artois makes no more delay but takes the large and heavy silver plates again and the two girls went crying: "Loyal loves lead us which go enchanting us." Robert has called a brave knight - it was John de Beaumont, a conquering prince, uncle to the gentle count of Hainault, the powerful - and said to him very gracefully: "Vow to the heron, sir, I pray you." John de Beaumont said: "Sir, at your will; but I marvel much at so much talk. Boasting is worth nothing unless it is accomplished. When we are in taverns, drinking the strong wines and the ladies are near who look at us drawing their kerchiefs round their smooth necks, their grey eyes smiling, resplendent with beauty, nature provokes us to have desire in our hearts to contend, looking for mercy as the result. Then we conquer Yaumont and Aguilant and others conquer Oliver and Roland. But when we are in the fields, on our swift war-horses, our shields at our necks and our spears lowered, and the great cold numbs us all, our limbs fail us both behind and before, and our enemies are approaching towards us, then we should wish to be in a cellar so great that we should never make a vow of one kind or other. For such boasting I would not give a besant. I do not say this as a ground to excuse myself for I vow and promise on the true body of St Amant that if the English king were to do so much as to enter in Hainault and pass Brabant and go through Cambresis to enter France, I will be his marshal to conduct his host to make war in France upon the powerful, rich king, and that I will not fail him for any man living, and in all his needs I will always be before him though I shall lose my land and all I am worth. But if the King of France would do so much as voluntarily to recall me into France from which I am banished as I am well aware, I would quit Edward so honestly, by God almighty, that no one, great or small, could point to me as acting injuriously or that I was grieving him by any treason. And if he does not so, I make a covenant to God that I will always be aiding the good King Edward and throughout the war I will be the leader of his people." And when the King hears him he thanks him.

When John de Beaumont had spoken his mind Robert of Artois did not delay: he has taken up the two dishes again and raised them. The three minstrels did not forget, the two girls sing, each led away one. Robert knelt before the queen[17] and said that he would distribute the heron in time after she had vowed her heart's thoughts. "Vassal," said the queen, "now speak to me no more: a lady cannot make a vow because she has a lord. If she vow anything her husband has power to revoke fully what she has vowed. And shame be to the person that thinks of it before my dear lord has commanded me."

The king said: "Vow, my body shall acquit it, but that I may accomplish it my body shall labour. Vow boldly and God will aid you."

Then the queen said: "I know well and have felt for some time that I am pregnant: it is only a little while since the child moved in my body. I vow and promise to God who created me, who was born of the Virgin while her body remained perfect, and who died, crucified, on the cross, that my body shall not bear fruit, until you have led me to the country over there to perform the vow that your body has vowed. And if I am ready to give birth when it will not be wanted I shall kill myself with a great knife of steel, my life will be lost and the baby will die."

When the king hears this he thought very seriously about it and said: "Certainly, no one will vow more."

The heron was divided and the queen ate of it. Then after this was done the king made his preparations and caused ships to be stored, the queen entered, and led many free knights with him. From there to Antwerp the King made no halt and when they had finished their voyage the queen was delivered and gave birth to a graceful, fair son. He was called Lion of Antwerp when they baptised him.[18] Thus the noble lady acquitted her vow: before they are all acquitted many a good man will die for it, and many a good knight will lament, and many a good woman will be tired of it. Then the English court went over there.

Here end the vows of the heron.

NOTES

1. Robert of Artois came to England 'towards the end of 1336' (Perroy 1951, p. 93), a much more likely date than 1338 by September of which year Edward III had already been in France for two months. On 5 September 1338 Edward III and the Emperor Lewis met in the marketplace at Coblenz (Wright 1859, p. xvi; Perroy 1951, p. 101).

2. Robert of Artois (d.1342) was descended from Louis IX (r. 1226-1270), and was married to a sister of Philip VI (r. 1328-50). Denied inheritance in Artois by successive Capetian kings, Robert resorted to forgery of documents and was accused of poisoning his aunt, the Countess Matilda in 1331-2. He fled France initially to Flanders and subsequently to England (Wright 1859, pp. x-xi). He was welcomed by Edward III, who also felt unjustly deprived of inheritance by Philip VI. Paradoxically, since 1316 the Capetian kings and Philip VI had favoured female succession in Artois, against the interests of Robert, while excluding females and those whose claims came through the female line from inheriting the throne of France.

3. The significance of references to Philip VI as 'clear faced', as here, or 'blear-eyed' as in the 'Invective', below, is lost.

4. Edward III's vow. The invasion plan described here was that which he followed in general terms, through the north of France in 1338.

5. Presumably the homage performed in 1329 at Amiens.

6. See above, Introduction to Minot, 'The Poet and the Court of Edward III.'

7. William de Montacute, Earl of Salisbury, 1337-44. The Earl of Salisbury is known to have been blinded in one eye in the Scots wars, and so this vow is unlikely. However, Froissart alludes to vows taken by young English 'bachelers' who promised

to wear patched eyes until they had performed some feat of valour.

8. Earl of Derby's daughter. For Henry of Grosmont (b. 1310, d. 1361), Earl of Derby, see Poem V, line 41 note. Grosmont had married Isabella Beaumont only in 1330. Contemporaries would have seen the implied joke here, the child and the half blind Montacute, old enough to be her father.

9. Walter de Mauny. See Poem V, line 39 note. Froissart describes the capture of Mortaigne, before which event Mauny confided to his companions that he had made a vow 'in England, before ladies and lords' and intended to carry his vow out at Mortaigne (Wright 1859, p. xvii). A modern commentator (Taylor 1987, pp. 238-9) suggests that Mauny's attack on Godemar de Fay's town was a fiasco.

10. See note 8 above.

11. Louis of Nevers, Count of Flanders (1324-46). This is a curious vow as Robert of Artois had been spurred on to reopen his claims to Artois in 1324 when female relatives of Louis of Nevers had been set aside in favour of Louis by Robert of Bethune (Perroy 1951, p. 92). There may be a further element of humour here, which suggests that the chivalrous knights were unable to distinguish their friends from their foes. However, Louis did oppose English activities in Flanders, was driven out, and eventually died at Crecy fighting for France.

12. Robert de Ufford, Earl of Suffolk (1337-69).

13. King of Bohemia. See Poem IV, line 67 note. A possible further tilt at the courtiers here. The King of Bohemia, selected as Suffolk's target, had actually saved the earl's life in 1340. Suffolk was captured in 1340, and but for the intervention of the King of Bohemia, who suggested that the captured earl could be exchanged for a peer of France, would have been executed by Philip VI.

14. John de Beaumont (d. 1342) was married to a sister of the Earl of Derby. The various relationships of the Beaumont family within the European aristocracy are clouded with uncertainty.

15. The capture of Suffolk alluded to here dates the composition of the poem presumably to after that event, hence the comments about the King of Bohemia.

16. Jean de Faukemont. Leader of 'free companies', who were well known for their unrestrained behaviour outwith the chivalric code.

17. Queen Philippa of Hainault (d. 1369), wife of Edward III. Her father, Count William I of Hainault, was married to Joan, a sister of Philip VI of France, which made Philippa the King of France's neice.

18. Lionel of Antwerp (b. 1338, d. 1368 in Milan) was the fifth child and third son of Edward III. He became Duke of Clarence in 1362.

Appendix 2

Here we present translations of four Latin poems nearly contemporary with those of Laurence Minot. These poems demonstrate that a patriotic and chauvinistic element was by no means peculiar to Minot's verse. They are arranged in chronological order, in the cases of the first three on the dates of the events to which they refer. This does not prove that they were written in that order. In the cases of the second and third pieces (the 'Invective' and 'Neville's Cross'), four distinctive lines are found in both, which at least suggests the authors (assuming there was more than one) were aware of the existence of the other poem. In the case of the fourth poem, the date of *c.* 1350 is assigned on the basis of its codicological environment in Ms. Cotton Titus. A. xx. First there is an epigram which very concisely articulates the basis of Edward's claim to the throne of France (1340). The epigram refers to 1339 in the original, but this has been changed here to 1340 because Edward actually assumed the arms of France at Ghent in January 1339/40, new-style 1340. This is followed by 'An Invective against France' (post-dating the battle of Crecy, 26 August 1346) and then a poem on the battle of Neville's Cross (17 November 1346). The fourth poem is 'The Dispute between an Englishman and a Frenchman,' which probably dates to *c.* 1350. The original of the epigram is in Ms. Rawlinson 214. The poem on Neville's Cross is in British Museum Ms. Reg. 13 A. xviii. 'An Invective against France' and 'The Dispute between an Englishman and a Frenchman,' and are both in Ms. Cotton Titus A. xx., (the 'Invective' is also in Ms. Bodl. 851 and Ms. Rawlinson 214).

These poems are by no means the only Latin pieces which deal in some detail with political and military events of the period *c.* 1340-1350 from a patriotic English point of view. Three of the manuscripts mentioned above contain other such pieces, certain of which are found in common between the three. Topics covered include the battles of Crecy and of Neville's Cross (this time in a long version), and the truce of 1347, as well as subsequent events such as the Spanish expedition of 1367, which culminated in the Black Prince's victory at Najera. All of these poems are edited by Thomas Wright in *Political Poems* (1859) and we have used his texts as the basis of our translations. Certain words have defied translation and where this is the case indication is given in the text thus, [......]. Other editorial interventions are similarly offered in square brackets.

Although it is the case that these poems present a view of events which shares the ethos of Minot's lyrics we should not be misled into thinking that this necessarily constitutes evidence for the generalised growth of national feeling and patriotic solidarity. It shows only an interest in such ideas among a courtly and literate circle. Furthermore, literature, especially literature with such a strong emphasis on national politics and values, should probably be seen as prescribing rather than describing appropriate ways of thinking and thus it might even be said that such explicitly propagandist pieces indicate a perceived need to stimulate a national impetus which was not being adequately maintained.

I. Epigram on the Assumption of the Arms of France, 1340

The Right of Edward King of England in the Realm of France.

I am king of the two realms for a twofold reason. I regard myself a King of England by right deriving from my father. I am indeed styled King of France by right on my mother's side. Hence come my two coats of arms in the year 1340.

APPENDIX 2

II. An Invective against France

France, womanish, pharisaic, embodiment of might, lynx-like, viperish, foxy, wolfish, a Medea, cunning, a siren, cruel, bitter, haughty, you are full of bile. She offers honey but skulks like a snake in the grass. Led by Philip Valois, surnamed the blear-eyed [......]. You are too arrogant, uncherished by the warmth of love, tainted with deceit, despised, refreshed by inflicting horror. You look to Philip Valois to be your blear-eyed king. Your feet run to the mark [......]. Philip the barbarian has corrupted the judge's jurisdiction, Philip has attacked the mighty sceptre of the realm. You look for an heir: Philip is not your heir. You bring about many battles: the greater is the number of wounds you will suffer.

Edward III, the English boar and leopard, is your true king. Coming against you with cruel fangs he has crushed your heart, annexed your goods and brought much beneath his sway. He has finished off the wars, shattered the strongholds and restored the laws. Depart, Philip, you blear-eyed invader of the realm. You look askance like blear-eyed Agrippa. *Phy* stinks, a blear-eyed man offends with his eyes and, therefore, Philip offends and stinks and will reap a squalid destiny.

Philip Valois, Xerxes, Darius, Bituitus: Edward, the wily boar will make you ill. Often famous kings have relied too much on numbers. They have been defeated by small forces, taken prisoner and died in chains. Though we are a small force we recover by taking thought. When our hearts are arrogant and we take on airs then we perish. The unjust take up arms and, for many, justice is in retreat. They take up arms, they trust in God, justified by the facts and by their reputation. When you make a show of genuine peace and conceal your deceit you fan the flames of war and honour is lost. You have brought many into subjection not by force but by a wolf's cunning. You fled from the boar: your strength is like the hoar frost. The wild beast attacks you, the famous king harries you with the sword. He is left with his fame: your folly brings you disgrace. You are made soft by fear while integrity distinguishes the boar.

Justice gives him heart: you lose heart through your injustice. This peerless boar, dweller in the forest, sharp and bold, with his splendid shoulders, aims deadly points at you. France, like the kites, shows that she will be a Scylla. The boar king comes from the forest and puts an end to her. Death is brought to the people of Paris by the boar's teeth. His teeth are sure, clean, strong and sharp. As long as the boar lives and rules his realm wisely England gives out light while God gives the boar his sharpness.

If you are worth anything Valois, put away fear. Show yourself in the field, stand fast, display your energy. you are the flower, you have lost the flower, in the field your strength has dried up: *Mane, Tegel, Phares*. You show yourself a wolf and a lynx, not a lion. The lynx sees just as well from afar, he pretends, he plots. He sets a long-lasting ambush during which he does nothing. The lynx gives you his sight but the lion does not give you his might. In any case, a king can use might without sight. Were you to lay aside your might and put on deceptive looks, a king seen but unseen, you would soon have no sight. You are an indoor flower, in war you are like a girl. Your hopes lie in deceit and you make for the safe places.

Valois, steeped in filth, fix your teeth once more in your delights. Bite like a woman, or scratch, heartless man. Suppose you are a man with the heart of a king, compassionate, true, merciful; yet your mind is corrupted by your filth and degrades you. Why will you wickedly bring out your mighty royal bodyguards ? You are stripped of them and so no longer regarded as a king. Show yourself a king or give up the title. Your surname is Valois, your family are monsters. You collected money, you pretended to be going on a pilgrimage, you spent your ill-gotten gains to no profit, you attacked the dowry of Christ and did not prevail. In sorrow you will restore to me what you held. The treaty I made by bringing the war to an end you broke in your folly. You went into hiding, you turned tail and fled. You started battles and appointed the times and places. You made a show of legality. You ran away. You were beaten and departed. You practised deceits, you observed no truces. You broke down bridges. You destroyed the bridges of the law. You are a destroyer of the bridge of life and an inspirer of terror. You are a wicked extortioner, a make-believe conqueror of the realm. You refused the title of priest, you abused the title of king, aimless with friends who lack integrity. We miss Oger, Karl, Roland and Oliver. Your heart is as a hare's foot, the boar makes you act like a hare. On his own ground the boar will soon say to you "checkmate". You will not say "leveret": you are a hare. He is a boar and would become one to you. What seems to be pure gold you pretend is the Minotaur. It is the realm, your treasure, not the laurel that you mind losing [......].

Why do you run ? Stand here, Philip, stand up to the boy. Depend on yourself: why do you fight like a sophist ? This boy here will show you finer flowers. You pretend to have burning ambition but look: the boar is robbing you of your honours. The boar takes their sacrificial garlands from the heads of the French and gives them arrows remitting the accepted punishment of Jacob and Jonathan. O ! the wonderful arrow that preserves the good, attacking cunningly ! You will aim for fearsome and sharp targets. The good spirit that breathed on you has left you, Saul: it has passed to David, inspiring success in battle. Edward is David. He glistens with holy unction. Philip, who has lost his courage is Saul, reluctant to join battle. The boar is Edward, flower of kings, pure ointment, the only sun that shines, rose of the world, our guiding star. He is the world's treasure, its heart, its example. A garland of gold or roses is justly his due. See, his help is God, because he is noble like Maccabaeus, uttering devout praises and to him Jeremiah gives a sword. The sword is honed, easy to handle and gold-mounted. It will swiftly conquer the land of the French and drive them out.

So small a prince, a pebble hacked from a mountain will cut into pieces, crush and squeeze a mighty statue in obedience to God. The natural world knows none superior to him. He inflicts terror and intolerable hardship on the French. This king is all-powerful, he is more valuable than any gold. He is laid on a cross and scorched by fiery breath. He bears the shields of hope, faith, piety and love so that all the time he is planning a peaceful outcome. With such a shield goes the sharp sword of passion. He urges war unharmed since he has cast down the mute devil. Not without due reflection does he confront innumerable foes, starving and thirsty, enduring cold and brutality.

We sleep in safety though he rarely sleeps. We cross over in safety for he discharges a shower of arrows. For us he gives his all, his heart, his body, his money. He roars like a lion and frightens away stern spirits. Therefore, because he undertakes such great tasks on our behalf and devotes himself to us, we give him our love. Therefore let us give him our land, our money, our hearts, our bodies, our devotion. In the power of God let us do honour to this great hero. He is a defence to us, bravery, courage and freedom from fear, a good King Arthur, filling the French with sorrow. The boar's teeth will be cudgels against the Parisians. The leopard king is justly the King of Paris. Let us who are justly made his sons and have earned the fruits of a just war be grateful to him. He reigns as the sole man of honour. The garlic blushes, the leopard's lilies grow. They wilt of themselves, the leopard's realm is conquered and peaceful. The garlic is in confusion, the leopard's realm trembles.

Let law and peace be preserved. The French are groaning in their hearts. Once I was led astray as a young king and brought across the sea, persuaded by trickery. But by the grace of Christ I was saved and I made over a fief to Philip according to the custom of the younger sort. When older I broke it with the full approval of my people. If a young man is wronged there will be redress as the law requires. Therefore let me be given what the gross Philip possesses. I feel that I have been wronged, Philip Valois: you are evading justice. With Jesus in my heart I shall dispute successfully with you. Help will come to a minor who is the victim of deceit and trickery. France will be handed over to me who was sick and led astray. The law's decision makes me heir to France. Why then do you befoul my throne by taking the title of king ? On you, my kinsman, there are no marks of kingship.

APPENDIX 2

Therefore promptly yield up to me your position in the name of
the law. You are not healing the royal malady, you are
profaning the realm. That your lineage be not vain, heal your
timid heart. It is a great malady should the king's heart be
weak as a lamb. Therefore he should properly have the heart of
a lion or of an eagle. When Clovis, the first King of France,
was re-born he was anointed with oil brought down from the
heights of heaven. That was preserved and with it the King of
France is customarily anointed. By a strange destiny Valois
cannot take his turn. The lack of the oil proves you will not
be king. Therefore, acknowledge this: abandon your flock and
seek after God. There was nothing in the flask so there is no
anointing for you. Your soul is black, draw your cowl close.
The King of Kings has come and within he pityingly makes the
rough places smooth. Therefore there is no longer any
anointing from a similar vessel for France.

France is owed to Edward. Watch out, blear eyes ! Should a
banquet be prepared the boar will hear of it: therefore, watch
out. The boy will, by force, deprive you of your strength:
therefore, watch out. The boy will, by force, deprive you of
your senses: therefore, watch out. If you are the true king
protect the crown of France. Play the part of king, we want
none of Homer's tales. Don't play the hare lest France destroy
her honour and lose the flower which is the perfume of the
king's standard. You have a numerous nation but their hearts
are buried deep and dried up. Their fear is great indeed. They
know nothing of the ways of Mars, thirsting for blood they get
drunk like raw recruits and are defeated in the terrible
strife.

God is with him to guide him, the law is with him, popular
support is with him. Deceit and trickery are with you, the law
is not with you, flight is with you. With him is nobility of
soul, popular support, justice towards all. With you is the soul
of a mouse, pitiable, slippery and blind. Therefore, with the
favour of God, with might supporting his strength, with justice
as his aim, he hopes to defeat Goliath: "The Lord is with me,
no battles shall harm me. Fighting hand to hand the joyful
French shall turn to weeping."

The foolish troops of France are many. May the King of Kings direct the infantry and cavalry of England. Sing unto the Lord, sing Valois, Lord Sardanapalus. Trick their leaders, trick them, you will utterly defeat the French. The elephant fighting on a hill with a rhinoceros wears his heart on his brow. Your heart is where a chameleon wears his. You turn your back to him, you turn and face backwards. Get down low like a pig that has been badly bitten. You are a clerk in the closet, you know nothing of battle. You lie down like a snake on its belly, a mouse, a dormouse. It is no ordinary boar you feed on and you will be taken prisoner. You will be slain by the sword that preserves him and you will be stained with blood. It is not the sword of justice or religion or virtue that you carry from the battle you who paint frightful cruelty. You will be struck by a dark sword, heart facing upwards. You lose your lion's heart and are wrapped in a sheepskin.

By the law of France the realm is denied to a woman. The supreme sovereign issued decrees in contradiction. The former law was made under the butcher Capoth [i.e. Capet]. Therefore such a law was recently abrogated in lordly fashion. The former law was the work of Hugo Capoth the butcher. The latter law, its handmaiden, is fittingly bereft of friends.

He changed his name and took the name Pipinus. Shrewd and foxy, he abrogated the law of the lord. The royal heiress to France married Pipinus and lived as queen of her people by divine dispensation. Her proud husband, to whom she paid too much regard, a stupid, ungrateful fellow, undistinguished and with charges laid against him, agreed to a law which provided that no woman thereafter should succeed a king or exercise royal authority. If the butchers of the flock made the laws for their own people, then the the whirlwind would not touch the kings of those realms. Clearly, the butcher's law is in opposition to the wise word of God and, therefore, it will be consigned to perdition. The word of God is that Salphays, the fifth daughter, makes good her claim to be legally recognised as her father's heiress. Their demand is just, right, clothed in reason, valid, popular, and approved by the word of God. The law being submitted to the Lord by the king provides that when a king dies, if he had a good title in law, the heir is his son. If the male line fails, a daughter succeeds her father. If there is no daughter, the succession will be conferred on a brother. The law does not discriminate therefore do not discriminate. Deceit does not render void the due laws of heaven. Therefore the law must apply to dukes, kings and commons.

The heart of France is numbed, there is no rich harvest. Isabella, mother of our king, a lady noble, wise, beautiful, whose virtues shone like the stars, beloved daughter of Philip, King of France, had married the King of England: a sure road to peace. His three brothers died without issue. The law, God and the council granted her the rights of the realm. Whatever legal right the mother has, she rightfully passes to her offspring. The offspring do not fade into obscurity but fulfil their mother's gift. Christ is King of the Jews by succession to his mother. Therefore, let the boar become King of France by succeeding his mother. The Duke of Normandy is king by succeeding his ancestors; the conqueror of Scotland by personal conquest and the lives of his men. The Emperor Charles, a king of noble lineage, a tyrant, taught by heaven as soon as he was drawn from the womb, heard it said, in the answer given to Ludwig, that his daughter whom he was to beget would reign as king. She reigned with her mother's name but by right derived from her father. Therefore in this matter let us believe the noble Ludwig.

Therefore, Count Philip, give the boar his due rights. She too will come who will be a stern, awe-inspiring countess. At last, Duke, make your lament, you who have caused so much havoc and hand over the realm of the leader who is the light of the world. Spare the bloodshed, spare the pain, spare the cruelty, spare the shame, spare the toil: you are already sparing honour. Let it be your noble aim to give true answers as to the pains you have taken to administer my rights. You will not be able to make restitution because there is not enough money. Therefore, should you come in repentance, you will come upon forgiveness.

APPENDIX 2

Realm of England, rose of the world, flower without thorn, honey without dregs: you have won the war at sea. The French ships hurtled to their destruction like birds flying into a net. They streamed with blood, used to soft living they missed their beds. See, the English graveyard makes mincemeat of the French. They perish, they toss about, they are at their wits ends, they take to flight. Chaan the offspring of Chanaan was despatched by Edward Carnarvon whom he was attacking.

Tell how few here showed loyalty, virtue or honour. Tell of panic, blundering, and the promise of mourning. Tell how here the flower of France fell. Here the famed King of England worsted us. At Crecy the fame of England grew. France wept, grew small, raged, took to flight as the habit set in. Three brave kings ranged against us. Two of them soon fell though they did not deserve death. A luckless king fell grievously afflicted. In marvellous fashion his destiny shows him the zest of the English. He got no benefit then form royal birth. He had the title of king but no advantage in reality. The King of Bohemia, who surpassed the most eminent in the nobility of his lineage, a man shrewd and full of years, fell ingloriously at Crecy. Blind he surely was in entering blindly into the battle. He sought fame but lost control. Third to run forward was a king who roared like a lion in a painting. He was like a lion in his boasting, like a hare in his scampering from the field. Barons, counts, nobles, and infantry were chased by the English infantry and slain as they fled.

The battle, King, surpassed human understanding. Therefore pray to God the dues for the end of the campaign. King, give your heart to Christ, guide your heart by reason, reconcile all hearts to yourself, unite the hearts that strive against one another. Be thankful to God who has accomplished wonders for you. Be not arrogant, bless him who created all things. Benhadad formed a league of thirty-two noble kings and the soft-hearted Ahab overcame them. Look at Sennacherib, grieve for Nebuchadnezzar, Amaziah, Antiochus, Pharoah, Saul, Uzziah. These became too proud and railed against the Lord. Kings that they were they were blown up in their own conceit and perished.

King, keep the loins, the eyes, the mouth, the heart on the
straight path, protect the temples. Cause yourself, the nobles
and the commons to hold fast the bidding of Christ. Trusting in
Christ, smiling in the name of Christ, watching yourself, your
gains and losses, be a spear whistling through the air to land
on the French. Look on us with thy favour, O Christ. The humble
have overcome the proud, the meek peacemakers have overcome
the stern and bitter. Poverty has triumphed over riches and
weakness over strength. Therefore may the poor prosper by good
fortune. May plague, treachery, panic, insolence all give way to
peace.

King, well done ! Live with a pure heart. Mighty France made
a fearsome conspiracy against us but has drawn back. The sea
has drawn back. The waters afford you passage. Our nation has
passed over unharmed: there were no waves. Leading us
wonderfully, Jesus becomes our way. Therefore by such a path
we cross in safety and continue. Let us unite ourselves with
the Lord in especial zeal. One man routs a thousand and two
men rout ten thousand. They were fired by a spirit which these
lacked. They were brought to fulfilment by the Lord who sold
the others. Weak as we are the power of Christ revealed us as
his. When honour and love, fear and hope are gone then you
will perish. If you have genuine love you will walk in safety
at all times. May you be united by hope, courage and love,
touched by fear, anointed by honour, so that language does not
part us nor wound us.

Valois, cruel, piratical, scarce ever to be trusted, our arms
have deprived you of ships and sails. Enemy of our fleet, often
the scourge of our sailors, where are your exploits now ? What
strength is displayed ? Many are those you took prisoner,
murdered and plundered. Therefore, may the curse of Christ
visit you to your cost. Bitter as bile, you keep honey in your
mouth. You will suffer, you get your deserts according to the
law. Soon you will be confounded, burnt and done away with.

King, do not spare them. Search the inner rooms and the
strong boxes, confiscate the pounds and marks and do not be
generous in returning them. England laments that honour and

love are being buried. True loyalty is dying: laws, fame and peace are not to be found. She is unfairly assessed, stripped of her wealth, crushed, downtrodden and scoured clean though labouring under a burden of grief. England, once you lay exhausted by a great weariness; now you have risen in value and shimmer like the scales of a fish. Often a trader knows his work is wearisome but thinks it attractive because of the profit. If you choose the work of a king and live by the rule of the law then put up with the damage to your flock because you make a threefold gain.

What is better than this title ? What more attractive than a good prospect ? Your celebrated king will give you a famous name. In earlier times you were in bad odour and had a title of ill repute: now under him you have earned a title of great celebrity. Your bow and your destiny are known to the whole world. Suppose there is power in a pious prayer, then your merit is your title. You rejoice in a title, you are respected, you are enobled. You acquire an unrivalled reputation on sea and land.

Angelic English Edward, friend of the right, be a peacemaking king, long-suffering, devout, pure, just, generous, merciful, restrained, cheerful, truthful, dignified, approachable like Godric. With the Lord at his side, let the king be joyful, prudent, dedicated to Christ, liked by the people, known to you. Be generous to the common people, wise, with as many eyes as Argus. Believe in Christ, avoid worldly deceit. Trust in Christ. Smile in the name of Christ. Be a spear whistling through the air to land on the French.

Truces come in a treacherous manner from the face of the lamp. King, beware of truces, lest you perish by them. Pure-minded king, well blessed in virtuous lineage, trust in the teaching of your own people, Judah. Through his own people he wins the honour of victory. United in friendship with Rome, the compact is sealed as custom requires. Act, command, enjoin, endure, do good, lead well, bless. You are Lucifer, bring blessings, gather up the crops of France. Men hate a king who thinks only of income, a fool, an unjust man. They love a gallant, just and sensibly generous one. Keep Christ's commandments, fear and love him well. It is an unattractive race that loves this world. Piously honour the law, your flock and peace. Let God's praise sound sweetly and the words of your lips be godly.

Let France weep. She has been beaten like the Picts. May all the blessed saints pray for us. The humble English nation, devout, poor and without might has triumphantly beaten France and shed her blood. Therefore let God be rich and the King of England poor. Fortune is at your side, England, stand fast in Christ and you shall live. Saint Omer becomes very dear to our king. The glorious saint turns bitter towards his own people.

Christ, King of Kings, may this good king of ours find favour with you. Be to him the hope of life when you say "Go ! Come !" In all things may Christ be his defence, his ruler, his guide, his thought, his glory, his comfort.

Amen.

III. On the Battle of Neville's Cross

If you are worth anything, Valois, put aside fear. Stay in the field, be obedient, display your energy. You are the flower, you have lost the flower, your strength has dried up: *Mane, Techel, Phares*. You are a horse, a lynx: you do not look like a lion. France is the flower of flowers, the capital once of those of nobler birth. Now, against his nature, the leopard carries off the honours. I supply the flower, I seize the glory of him that prospers. Once I was the flower: now I fear the real beast with its splendour.

Edward was born in Windsor and trained to arms, a lucky king, up to now called upright. He is a great-hearted warrior, loyal and utterly trustworthy. He is not two-faced and is without stain throughout all the world. He gladly endures much hardship for the sake of his rights. Under so mighty a commander town and countryside are safe. Near Berwick he has overcome an enemy nation and shows that he will be a friend to the English and earn them praise.

Marvelling at the nations as they fall by the sword of Halidon Hill he praises them as they run, fleeing with swift feet. Then Scotland has suffered a defeat full of sorrow. She realises that Edward's luck will still cause her to mourn. At Durham you would have been weeping if you could have seen the grim warfare. Fallen were the nobles, fallen fathers and fallen sons and heirs. Many Scots fled, many died. Those kept their lives who were taken prisoner and paid ransom. David Bruce will not forget this battle. He was wounded, defeated and captured. Blessed be the king.

IV. The Dispute between an Englishman and a Frenchman

The Frenchman speaks:

England, shit of men, shame of the world, ultimate evil, guiltier than all this, what do you do to make yourself guilty ? With what language, foul as pitch, do you assail the air ? With what weapon do you assail the air ? What thunderbolt do you launch from your mouth ? Your speech takes over your thoughts and licks filth from your heart. It clots and the venom of your thoughts flows from your mouth. The corruption of the root spreads into the branch and from it the whole nation gets its villainy. You corrupt everything, you are the mentor, you make it a reproach, you degrade the banner of virtue into vice.

You reproach me with well-dressed hair, pale cheeks, soft speech, and a controlled, civilised gait. If a sense of order controls the hair and insists it be neatly dressed a shambling step would be an abandonment of principles. If my face is pale, it is Pallas who spreads the pallor over my features and this complexion does not come from Venus. If I utter soft sounds, it is because what was at first a harsh sound to the ears makes the words acceptable when softened in the mouth. If my walk is, at first, with delicate steps this is because my outward restraint controls also my inner self. Each neat trait is brilliant and the brilliance is that of my innermost and outermost being alike: my outward appearance is the product of my inner nature. But because it is not markedly distinguishable from vice, virtue has often incurred reproach.

You also charge us with meanness because we show restraint and refuse to be slaves to our gullets and nothing else. What creatures does England rear except cattle ? Their belly is their God and it is to the belly that they gladly offer sacrifice. The wasteful glutton fills his gullet and stretches his stomach. He swells up and is more beast than man. To provide him with drink the very ponds are planted with crops: these are two different elements and from their union nothing is produced. We drink the liquor of the vine: the lees are sold to England. As it is liquid they think it is the liquor. You drink the lees but only at feast times - and then it is sparingly doled out to a few. However, if you swallow anything in accordance with the rite of Lyaeus, it is proper to mark the feast of God with this chant: "Hail festival day, worthy of honour throughout all ages, day on which God enters the blood and sustains us from without."

The Englishman speaks:

I should like to know why the Frenchman presses me to fight and what effrontery prompts you to speak, Frenchman ? What menaces lower from your brow ? What threats rumble in your chest ? What are your lips up to with their smooth utterance ? Leave the men alone, let woman strive with woman: unequal is a man's struggle with a woman. Whatever posture you take, wherever you go, there is always some element to bring you reproach. Should you look at her head while she preens herself with her neat hair she involves all the other men with some pretext or other. If she turns her head now to one side, now to the other, you will run off thinking she does not fancy you. If the vice of Venus robs your face of its colour, your fault is loudly proclaimed by your paleness. If your tongue softens its force so that your palate does not sound too loud then it is a woman talking through a man's lips. If your feet are swollen from walking you hold them in the air, scarce touching the road with the forward foot. If you surrender other parts to be used like a woman's you act like a woman and pretend not to be a man. If it is because a Frenchwoman is a castrated effeminate Frenchman then, Frenchman, take the name of French hen and the luck that goes with it.

Lest the only claim on Frenchmen is Venus and her ways, blind avarice has curved their grasping fingers. I will proclaim this reproach though it needs no saying. Be conviced by the evidence of a poor man's table. Bacchus saves some of the lees for the servants' table and the poor man's table is set with poor food. France harvest the chaff from the vine, England the grain. We drink off the the liquor, the Frenchman keeps the rest. Since such French depravity stains the soul of the Frenchman — Frenchman silence is best. Shut up !

Here ends a dispute between an Englishman and a Frenchman.

Appendix 3

Brief Table of Contents of Cotton Galba E. ix

f. 1a   Blank, on the verso the inscription *Chaucer, Exemplar emendate scriptum.*

f. 2   A leaf from a book of Hours.

f. 3a   Seven lines from the poem on the siege of Calais which is written in full at the end of the manuscript.

f. 4a   *Ywain and Gawain.*

f. 25a   *Ywain and Gawain* ends.

f. 25b   *The Seven Sages.*

f. 48b   A poem beginning 'Al es bot a fantum'.

f. 49a   'The Prophesies of Merlin'.

f. 50b   'Narracio de domino denario'.

f. 51b   A rood poem.

f. 52a   Poems of Minot.

f. 57b   'Hic incipit evangelium nichodemi'.

f. 67a   A poem on the seven deadly sins.

f. 69a   A poem on penance.

f. 73b   A metrical exposition of the Lord's prayer.

f. 76b   *The Prick of Conscience.*

f. 113b   Notes on horses, poem on the siege of Calais.

Select Bibliography

MANUSCRIPT

British Library

Cotton Galba E. Ix.

EDITIONS OF MINOT (In chronological order)

RITSON, Joseph, *Poems on Interesting events in the reign of Edward III written in the year MCCCLII*. With a preface, dissertations, notes and a glossary (London, 1795)

RITSON, Joseph, *Poems written anno MCCCLII by L. Minot* (London, 1825)

WRIGHT, Thomas, *Political Poems and Songs Relating to English History from the Accession of Edward III to the reign of Henry VII* (Volume 1, London, 1859)

SCHOLLE, Wilhelm von, *L. Minot's Lieder, mit grammatisch-metrischer Einleitung herausgegeben* (Strasburg, 1884). (In Brink, B. Ten and Scherer, W., *Quellen und Forschungen zur Sprach- und Culturgeschichte der germanischen Völker. Heft 52. 1874–1918.)

HALL, Joseph, *Poems of Laurence Minot* (1st ed., Oxford, 1887)

HALL, Joseph, *Poems of Laurence Minot* (2nd ed., Oxford, 1897)

CHILD, Francis James, *English and Scottish Popular Ballads* (Cambridge edition, Boston 1904)

HALL, Joseph, *Poems of Laurence Minot* (3rd ed., Oxford, 1914)

SELECT BIBLIOGRAPHY

STEDMAN, Douglas, *The War Ballads of Laurence Minot* (Dublin, 1917)

COLLETTE, Carolyn P., *The Poems of Laurence Minot* (Ph.D, University of Massachussetts, 1971)

SECONDARY WORKS

BARNIE, J. *War in Medieval Society. Social Values and the Hundred Years War* (London, 1974)

BENNETT, J.A.W. *Middle English Literature* (Oxford, 1986)

BRERETON, G. (ed.), *Froissart: Chronicles* (London, 1968)

COLEMAN, J. *English Literature and History 1350-1400* (London, 1981)

COTTLE, B. *The Triumph of English* (London, 1969)

Dictionary of National Biography, edited by Leslie Stephen and Sidney Lee (London, 1885-1900)

FOWLER, K. *The King's Lieutenant* (London, 1969)

GRANT, A. *Independence and Nationhood. Scotland 1306-1469* (London, 1984)

LEWIS, P. *Later Medieval France* (London, 1968)

McKISACK, M. *The Fourteenth Century, 1307-1399* (Oxford, 1959)

MOORE, S. 'Lawrence Minot' *Modern Language Notes*, xxxv (1920), pp.78-81

MORRIS, G.E. *Soldiers' Songs of the Thirteenth and Fourteenth Centuries* (Sheffield University MA Thesis, 1947)

SELECT BIBLIOGRAPHY

OAKDEN J.P. *Alliterative Poetry in Middle English* (Two volumes, Manchester, 1930 & 1935)

PALMER, J.J.N. *Froissart: Historian* (Woodbridge, 1981)

PEARSALL, D. *Manuscripts and Readers in Fifteenth-Century England* (Woodbridge, 1983)

PERROY, E. *The Hundred Years War* (London, 1951)

PRESTWICH, M. *The Three Edwards* (London, 1980)

SCATTERGOOD, V.J. *Politics and Poetry in the Fifteenth Century* (London, 1971)

SHERBORNE, J.W. and SCATTERGOOD V.J. *English Court Culture in the later Middle Ages* (London, 1983)

SISAM, K. *Fourteenth Century Verse and Prose* (Oxford, 1921, reprinted 1975)

TAYLOR, J. *English Historical Literature in the Fourteenth Century* (Oxford, 1987)

TURVILLE-PETRE, T. *The Alliterative Revival* (Cambridge, 1977)

WHITING, B. 'The *Vows of the Heron*', *Speculum*, 20 (1952), pp.261-278

WILSON, R.M. *The Lost Literature of Medieval England* (London, 2nd ed., 1970)

VALE, J. *Edward III and Chivalry* (London, 1982)

Index

N.B. Material cited in notes to the texts is not indexed here.

INDEX

St Omer, 56, 96
St Vaast-le-Hogue (Cotentin), 21, Poem VII, 43-8
Salisbury, Countess of, 18
Salisbury, Earl of, see Montacute
Scotland, 11, 15, 17-18, 20, 26-7, 53, 97
Shrewsbury, Battle of, 7
Sluys (later Flushing, Vlissingen), Battle of, 14, 17, 21, 38
Southampton (Hamton), 14, 17, 21, 32
Stirling (Striflin), 29
Stratford, Archbishop, 21
Suffolk, Earl of, see Ufford, Robert

Tournai, Siege of, 13, 21, Poem VI, 40-3
Trent, 52
Tweed, 52

Ufford, Robert de, Earl of Suffolk, 69, 77-8

Vermandois, 73
Vienne, Jean de, 51

Wallace, William, 19
Westminster, 52
Winchelsea, Battle of, 14-15, 17, 22, Poem X, 54-5
Windsor, 96

Yarmouth (Armouth), 32
York, Archbishop of, William de la Zouche, 52
Yorkshire, 8, 14
Ypres, 38

Zeeland (Seland), 32
Zwin (Swyn), Poem V, 37-40, 54